MOURNING *to* MORNING

90 Days of Healing After the Death of a Child

NANCY JAMES

Mourning to Morning: 90 Days of Healing After the Death of a Child

Contact the author at her Facebook page: www.facebook.com/pages/Mourning-to-Morning-by-Nancy-James.

Follow Nancy James on Twitter: @tnjames

Cover photography by Jérôme Brussee

Cover design by Yvonne Parks of www.pearcreative.ca

Publishing coordination by David Sluka at www.hitthemarkpublishing.com

Dedication and Thanks

This book is dedicated to you. I wrote this book to help mothers everywhere, in every nation, who have a child that has "gone away" to heaven. If I can survive the loss of a child, you can too. During my grieving process, I kept notebooks all over my house so I could write a prescription that would help others heal after the death of a child or any loved one. The book is easy to read all the way through. But then, put it near you and re-read one story a day. Let the Word work slowly through your soul.

I gave the first copy of this book to a friend whose son is named Jordan. I wrote it like we were having coffee together—discussing our children and our lives.

This book is also dedicated to my precious Tommy, and to Andrew, Bradley, Cameron, David, John Raul, Jordan, Lizabeth, Max, Robin, Shiloh, Timmy, Tony, Zander, and _____ (write in your own child's name).

I want to thank my amazing husband who walked through the Valley of the Shadow with a heart of integrity, faith, and wisdom. I want to thank, my three amazing kids—Julie, Jeremiah, and Mercy Lynn—who let me cry without reproof. Thank you for being patient while I wrote, which meant eating a lot of Pop Tarts and mac and cheese. I also want to thank Sugar Trask who spoke this book into being, and my mom who spoke encouraging words while I wrote.

A portion of the proceeds from this book will go to orphans in Zambia and to help women receive a new life after sex trafficking.

CONTENTS

1   THE LITTLE GIRL IS YOU 11

2   FEELING HAPPY AGAIN 13

3   MY SON IS GONE 15

4   THERE ARE NO POISONOUS JELLYFISH IN HEAVEN ... 17

5   I WAS AFRAID TO CRY 19

6   HOLD SORROW IN ONE HAND 21

7   LET'S BUY SOME EARRINGS 23

8   ONE CONTRACTION 25

9   THE GOOD SHEPHERD 27

10   DIALOGUING WITH GOD 29

11   YOU'RE NOT GOING CRAZY 31

12   SPECIAL FAVORS 33

13   IS IT OK TO ASK WHY? 35

14   JUST THE MENTION OF HIS NAME 38

15   IF YOU MISCARRIED 40

16   HEAVEN'S HALL OF FAME OF FAITH 42

17   A SHIELD OF FAITH 45

18   THE GRAVESTONE 47

19   SUFFERING 49

20	STAY ALIVE	51
21	DISHING IT OUT	53
22	DON'T GIVE ME THAT CRAP	55
23	LIFE SUPPORT	57
24	A BRIEF LIFE IS NOT AN INCOMPLETE LIFE	59
25	DOING WHAT YOU DREAD	61
26	DON'T PULL THE PLUG ON GOD	63
27	EVERY MOVEMENT	65
28	LONG DISTANCE TO HEAVEN	67
29	MARTHA'S FAITH	69
30	BUDDY AND SPARKY	72
31	OUR FATHER: THE PRODUCER AND DIRECTOR	74
32	LAUGHTER	76
33	KNOW FEAR = NO PEACE	78
34	NO FEAR = KNOW PEACE	80
35	NO FEAR FOREVER	82
36	ALL PRAISE FOR JOB	84
37	KEEP THE FAITH	87
38	SEX AND SUFFERING	89
39	HELPING THE HURTING	91
40	Y'ALL ARE GONNA BE TIRED	93
41	HOW KIDS HANDLE DEPRESSION	96

42	SWEET RELIEF	98
43	GOD IS NOT A JEALOUS GOD	100
44	ONLY JOB LOST IT ALL	102
45	YOU ARE LIKE MARY THE MOTHER OF JESUS	104
46	IF YOU TOUCH	106
47	RAW AND OPEN	108
48	I TOLD GOD I WAS ANGRY (BY JESSICA SHAVER)	110
49	PUSH! PUSH! PUSH!	112
50	HEALED STITCH BY STITCH	114
51	YOU ARE NOT RUNNING ALONE	116
52	HOW TO LET GO OF THE PAIN	118
53	EVERY DAY IS GREAT FAITH	120
54	WHEN YOUR HEART HAS BEEN SHATTERED	122
55	ERASER	124
56	POLLYANNA	127
57	ANTI-DEPRESSANTS	129
58	THE HEART WILL SPEAK	131
59	GOD CARES FOR YOU	133
60	GOD ISN'T PICKING ON YOU— MAYBE HE'S PICKING YOU OUT	136
61	WHAT IS HEAVEN LIKE?	139
62	WHY DO CHILDREN DIE?	141

63 WHAT IF YOUR CHILD COMMITTED SUICIDE OR OVERDOSED ON DRUGS? 143

64 WHEN GOD SAYS NO 145

65 CAMERON 147

66 MY STORY: AN ANGEL IS BORN 151

67 THE DARKEST CLOUD 153

68 I FELT LIKE I WAS LOSING MY MIND 155

69 OUR LITTLE VALENTINE 157

70 PRAYING FOR RESURRECTION AND LIFE 159

71 POWER TEAM 2 161

72 LEAVING FOR THE LAST TIME 163

73 ANGER IS A PRAYER 165

74 I'M SO MAD AT YOU! 167

75 HOW TO GET MAD AT GOD 169

76 IT IS GOOD 171

77 MY HEART IS SO BROKEN 173

78 SPINNING THE WHEEL OF FORTUNE 175

79 STAY AWAY FROM CRYSTAL BALLS 177

80 BITTERNESS 179

81 NOTHING IS AN ACCIDENT 181

82 I WAS THE WRECK 183

83 HOW TO BREAK STRONGHOLDS 185

84 SEPTEMBER 10, 2001 188

85   HOW MUCH ARE YOU WORTH?.......................191

86   FEELING BETRAYED BY GOD...........................193

87   WHO WILL LOVE THE KING?............................195

88   ON THAT DAY...197

89   REGRET AND UNRESOLVED ISSUES.............199

90   BE YOURSELF—HEALING IS HERE................201

     64 PRESCRIPTIONS FOR HEALING................204

     SIMPLE PRAYERS...217

THE LITTLE GIRL IS YOU

Close this book for a second and take a look at the picture on the cover. It would be easy to take a look at the cover and think that the little girl symbolizes a daughter. It does not. The little girl is you. Remember that each time you look at the cover and pick up this book.

God wants to bring you—a woman who has experienced a tragic loss—into a place of healing so that you can once again see the beauty of the morning. May this book help you in this process. "Weeping may last through the night, but joy comes with the morning" (Psalm 40:5 NLT).

At the end of each of the following readings there is one or more ways you can respond to help the healing process in your life. Many of the recommendations come from my own experience. I believe they will also help you.

At the end of this book I have also included sixty-four "prescriptions," which are activities you can do to speed along your healing.

Many of the daily readings have short prayers at the end. I have compiled all of these prayers at the end of this book. Print them out and use them as a reference to cast your cares upon the Lord.

Take a moment and look back at the cover one more time. This is you. Inhale. Exhale. Beauty and joy are coming for you in the morning. Let's walk your path of healing together.

FEELING HAPPY AGAIN

Have you had this experience? You awake from a nice sleep, lying in bed, without a care in the world. Suddenly, the reality of your situation hits you! You remember that there is a big hole in your life—your child is not with you. Slowly, the pain seeps back into your heart. But for three seconds, you enjoyed happiness as you once knew it.

Those three seconds are your hope for the future! You won't always feel the awful dread and pain that you feel now. You will feel happy again. I remember attending a welcome home party for a friend who had been a relief worker in Africa. She contracted malaria and came close to death but miraculously recovered. Three weeks after her recovery, her husband contracted the same disease and died! It was a big shock to everyone.

Several years had passed, she had remarried, and she came to the USA to celebrate. During the party, I couldn't get over how her joy was overflowing with radiance and laughter. I felt like I was dying in the desert, and she had the water that I longed so desperately to enjoy. As I was walking out to the car, my heart was bleeding. I cried out to God, "Am I ever going to be happy like her? Please, I want to be happy again; I hate being sad." When I called out to God in my desperation, I felt like a hand compressed the gaping hole in my heart.

I didn't think it would be possible to be happy again, but I asked God anyway. He said, "If you ask for bread, you will not get a stone." (See Matthew 7:9.). "Delight yourself in the Lord, and He will give you the desires of your heart" (Psalm 37:4 NASB). My desire was to be happy again. He also promised that if we have faith that is the size of a mustard seed, it could move mountains. (See Mark 11:23.) My mustard seed was my request to be whole again. Today I am more content, confident, peaceful, and faith-filled, than I ever was before my Tommy went to heaven.

I wrote this book so you could experience the same healing I experienced. I believe that if you try some of the prescriptions offered in this book, it will be a light leading you out of a dark tunnel. Ask God right now to be whole. Imagine yourself smiling and happy again.

MY SON IS GONE

If I need to refer to my child's death, I don't like to say, "We lost a child," because he is not lost! Tommy has found a beautiful Savior in the paradise in heaven. Instead, I say Tommy is gone. Tommy is away from us. We can no longer see Tommy, but he is alive and happy. Your child is the same cheerful guy or gal, except in a greater measure. They are not lost. "Lost" gives the impression of being gone forever.

Look at your child's absence as if they have gone away to college or graduate school. When a son or daughter leaves for college, there is great sadness because, realistically, things will never be the same as when they lived at home. Parents do have hope that eventually they will be reunited.

Because of our Savior, we have the hope of heaven. We have the audacious hope of being reunited with our children again. Everyday, I am anxious for that reunion. At first, I was more excited to see Tommy than I was about going to heaven. But the more I imagine heaven, the more I long for heaven's unveiling. I have an appointed time of death and I live life to the fullest while I am on earth.

What is heaven? In heaven, there is no more crying, no more pain. (See Revelation 21:4.) Heaven is the opposite of everything ugly and scary on earth. In heaven, there is no hunger, sadness,

And the wolf will dwell with the lamb,

And the leopard will lie down with the young goat,

And the calf and the young lion and the fatling together;

And a little boy will lead them.

They will not hurt or destroy in all My holy mountain,

For the earth will be full of the knowledge of the Lord As the waters cover the sea. (Isaiah 11:6, 9 NASB)

bullies, or smog. There is nothing fearful. Not only is there no sickness in heaven, but nothing dies.

There is no glass in the windows because there are no thieves! Even flowers can be picked and put in a vase, but they will never die! Our children won't ever get broken hearts or have broken promises! Wow!

What do you hate about earth? Write a list on this page and then encourage yourself that our children don't have to deal with any of these imperfections. All these things do not exist in heaven.

THERE ARE NO POISONOUS JELLYFISH IN HEAVEN

When I miss Tommy so badly that it hurts, which isn't very often anymore, I ask my Father God to do me a favor. I ask Him to give Tommy a gift from me—to tell Tommy that I am thinking about him. I've given Tommy ponies, orchards, beach houses, mountain cabins, rooms full of butterflies, and a party brimming with balloons.

This idea came to me while our family was on our annual Surfside beach trip. I was walking alone through the waves, and I wanted Tommy to be with us so badly that I could hardly breathe. I spoke to my Father: "Please give Tommy a beautiful day at a heavenly beach." Immediately, I looked down and saw a jellyfish. I believed God was telling me some very good news that I hadn't thought of before—there are no jellyfish in heaven. At least not the kind that sting! In fact, there is no evil, no pain, and no name-calling. Tommy will never experience a broken heart; he'll never get hurt in any way. That thought brought me a lot of comfort.

I like to think that Tommy and your child are friends, and that they are riding dinosaurs, surfing on sharks, and wading with whales. What fun they are having. One day, we'll be with them forever. But don't be in a hurry to get there. Impatience will spoil the process. Live your best on earth and that excellence will ensure your best days in heaven.

I've thought of a few wonders of heaven that our children will experience. List some of your own on this page. There are no boundaries in heaven. Everything is perfect. Be wild and creative! I'll give you a few hints. There is no gravity. There is no need for oxygen.

I WAS AFRAID TO CRY

A t first, I was afraid to let go and wail. I was afraid that I would fall off the slippery slope of sanity. I feared if I started crying, I wouldn't be able to stop. I didn't want to "go there." So I ignored the impulses to cry and grieve.

I specifically remember a fall day, when the urge to cry was extremely strong. I hesitated. It was 1:00 and the kids returned from school at 3:00. There was no way that I'd have enough time to cry and look presentable for the kids. It's funny now, but I remember being afraid that my kids would come home and find "the men in white suits" carrying their mom, in a straightjacket, into their van! But the prompting to cry was great, so I decided to jump into the icy waters.

I always started a crying session by calling out to the Father: "Catch me, lest I fall into a million smithereens." Then I let it out; I wailed and wailed. And when I was done, I looked at the clock— only twenty minutes had gone by! How was that possible? I felt my heart and discovered that it was true; it had been mended. My heart didn't feel tattered and torn as it had before I had prayed and cried.

"Crying is better than laughing. It blotches the face but it scours the heart" (Ecclesiastes 7:3 MSG). What I am about to say is crucial. I learned that to avoid a crying session is to avoid healing! Tears clean the soul. Tears release pressure and stress from our hearts. I hope you are just as amazed as I am at how quickly the Father can mend a heart. Just take His hand of peace. He wants to lead you on a walk. He has a plan to lead you out of the pain. Tears are the pathway to gladness. In the Amplified version, Ecclesiastes 7:3 says, "Sorrow is better than laughter, for by the sadness of the countenance the heart is made better and gains gladness."

Time doesn't heal. Time with God does. Healing doesn't mean you are forgetting your child. You will honor your child by healing. When you're healed, you can be productive and bring honor to your child's name. Your child doesn't want you to be a hot, stinking mess. Hold your Father God's hand, bury your face in His lap, and cry. It is the starting place of healing. I'm not afraid to cry anymore, but I don't let it rule my life or schedule either.

Have you allowed yourself to cry about your child, or do you hold it all in and try to keep it together? Keep reading, and I will help you through the mine field.

HOLD SORROW
IN ONE HAND

There is a wonderful little book called Hinds Feet on High Places by Hannah Hurnard. It helped me tremendously through the crying process. It is an allegory of a woman named Much Afraid. The Good Shepherd promises her a new life in the high places of the Kingdom. He says to her, "Whenever you are afraid, reach out and put one hand in Mine and the other hand in your journey partner's hand."

When He reveals that her journey partner is called "Sorrow," she breaks down and falls into a heap. The Good Shepherd brushes back her hair and tenderly says, "Now, Much Afraid, you promised to trust Me to pick the best companion for your journey. This companion will protect you from the evil one. Do you think I would make a mistake and pick something bad for you?"

---

[1] Hurnard, Hannah. *Hinds' Feet on High Places*. Blacksburg, VA: Wilder Publications, 2010. Print.

I was like Much Afraid most of my life. I was a miserable, wretched, bundle of fear. After Tommy died, if I felt tears coming on, I would reluctantly allow the tears while crying out to my Good Shepherd who would swoop down and hold my hand. I held on to Him for dear life!

When you feel sad, sit down, and in your mind, embrace the Good Shepherd in one hand and sorrow in the other. The pain won't be as intense. Don't do one without the other! You can't cry without Him, and He doesn't want you to ignore your pain. I'll be honest—it's messy, but it's worth the journey.

One time, I refused to hold the Good Shepherd's hand. Instead, I decided to hold Pity's hand. Pity tells you that you are all alone and no one has it as bad as you. (Hint: that is a lie.) I cried so hard and so long for three days that my Kleenex piled up three feet next to my bed. I did not clean it up as a "punishment" to God. I was a 35-year-old woman, acting like a three-year-old.

My six-year-old daughter came in my room, looked at my mess, and got a weird look on her face. "What's that?" she asked. I made excuses, but really it was Mommy's idol to self-pity! I was practically bowing down and worshipping it. When you hear Pity calling your name, call out to the Good Shepherd to protect you. It's ok to cry because we are sad and miss our kids. In fact, it's essential that you cry.

I recommend you read the book Hinds Feet on High Places. I think you will enjoy it. Go get a copy today. It will inspire you and encourage you on this new journey. I hope you know I am cheering you on!

LET'S BUY SOME EARRINGS

A fter a crying session, I felt a nudge from the Good Shepherd. He did the cutest thing. I felt prompted in my gut to go shopping—shopping for earrings! Many times after a crying session, I had the thought, "Come on; let's get some earrings." The Good Shepherd really knows the ways to a woman's heart! He didn't have to ask twice; I jumped in the car.

Why did He choose earrings? First of all, earrings are near and dear to my heart. They are the only jewelry that I wear, and they are the essence of my personality: gorgeous, and gaudy! I had my ears pierced a month after Tommy died because I wanted a permanent reminder of faith, hope, and love. There was momentary pain as I got them pierced, but then I had something beautiful in its place!

When Tommy died, my heart was pierced with momentary pain. Out of the process, the Good Shepherd put something beautiful in the place of the pain. Pain has preceded everything worth having in my life. In the situation with Tommy, I believed by faith that God was making something beautiful out of it.

Go shopping and pick up something as a faith-filled reminder to yourself. It can be a secret between you and the Good Shepherd. You may only see darkness today, but the dawn is coming! The Good Shepherd wants to carry you on His white horse to a place of contentment. It will come.

ONE CONTRACTION

In Lamaze classes, we were taught to focus on one contraction at a time. Don't imagine the totality of the labor, just focus on one contraction at a time. The coaches kept encouraging the "trainees" by reminding us that we could make it through one minute.

I used that same philosophy to live for one day. I got out of bed every day to live my best for that day. I lived one day at a time. It may sound corny, but it sure worked. I had three kids that needed a mom, and I had a husband that was working his butt off at his job. He didn't get the choice of staying in bed. The least I could do was get out of bed, eat breakfast, and take a shower. I have a standing motto: "Even though I feel like crap, I don't have to look like it!"

I want to encourage you to live for one day. Don't think about the totality of your life without your child. Live for one day. Do your best for one day. Cry when you feel like it, and then go get a manicure! After a wailing session, I always rewarded myself with a new pair of earrings, or I'd watch a chick flick, or I'd play with my kids. Become a kid again. Have fun to the best of your ability.

What do you like to do for fun? Go do it! Take your kids to some place fun that you rarely take them—like Disney World. I know indoor birthday playgrounds are loud and obnoxious, but your kids are suffering and need a little fun to work out their hurt and confusion. Pray for them that as they play, God will speak words of peace and comfort to them. Keep reading, and I will show you how to help your kids through the grieving process.

THE GOOD SHEPHERD

Isaiah 54:10–11, 13 says, "'For the mountains may move and the hills disappear, but even then my faithful love for you will remain. My covenant of blessing will never be broken,' says the Lord, who has mercy on you. '[Now you feel like a] storm-battered city, troubled and desolate! [But] I will rebuild you with precious jewels and make your foundations from lapis lazuli… I will teach all your children, and they will enjoy great peace'" (NLT, brackets mine).

Growing up, if your dad was too busy for you, you may have wrongly interpreted that God is too busy and has no time for you. If your dad was an angry person, you might think God is an angry God. Maybe you believe God will accept you if you do everything perfectly because your earthy dad was very demanding.

The reality is that you are already accepted and LOVED just because you are His child. Your relationship with God should be easy and full of fun! God is everything you have hoped, imagined, and ever dreamed Him to be. God says, "Come to me, all of you who are weary and over-burdened, and I will give you rest! Put on my teaching and learn from me. For I am gentle and humble in heart, and you will find rest for your souls. For my mission is easy and my burden is light" (Matthew 11:29 NASB).

Grab the Good Shepherd's hand in your mind's eye, and pray this "Prayer of Beginning": "God of Heaven, I choose this day to give You a chance in my life. I want to start believing that You are a merciful and kind God. I am sorry for thinking You were bad and mean. Thank You, that I don't have to be perfect or have it all together before You will love me. You love me just the way I am and just because I am Your child. Thank You God that You promise that if I draw near to You, You will draw close to me. Wrap Yourself around me, my husband, and my other children. Teach them Your ways and give them Your truth which is the foundation of real, lasting peace."

DIALOGUING WITH GOD

For a long while, the pain felt like a **shadow** that was following me. Then I remembered, "Yea, though I walk through the valley of the **shadow** of death, **I will fear no evil**" (Psalm 23:4 NKJV, emphasis mine). My Good Shepherd will protect and comfort me.

Then, during the course of the day, I dialogued with God, my Good Shepherd, just like He was my daddy. I had an honest relationship with Him. I asked a question and looked for an answer. Expect God to have a tailor-made prescription for your healing. Expect Him to whisper and to use people and experiences as His way of communicating. I wrote these special experiences of healing in a spiral notebook. I kept a different spiral in every room in the house! This book is a combination of those entries. I also kept a grateful journal. (Thanks, Oprah!)

The key to healing is practicing the presence of God—the Good Shepherd being with you. As you practice hearing the Good Shepherd's voice, get over the idea that you are crazy. If talking to

God is prayer, why is hearing from God crazy? I personally think God's a little sick of hearing us talk all the time; He's just too nice to say anything. So I'll say it for Him! Don't worry, if you're going crazy, someone you trust will tell you. Then you should seek professional help.

How do I know if an idea is from my God? Remember these three key words: smart, sweet, safe. It's a smarter idea than I could have created. It's a sweeter word than I would have said. It's a safe word. He won't tell me to hurt myself or someone else. I use the whispers as encouragement for my heart. I let the gentle whispers wash away my pain.

Find someone who has lost a child. They have been down this road, and there is nothing new under the sun. I found there were a lot of people who had lost someone special to them. I found out I wasn't alone. (Thanks, Dawn.)

The Psalms is a book of poems written from someone who was hurting but who trusted God. Find a Psalm that ends hopefully, and read it before you go to sleep tonight. Insert "depression," "hopelessness," or "fear" when it speaks about "the enemy." Some Psalms that would be good for this are 23, 34, 43, 46, 56, 61, 62, 63, 70, 71, 77, 84, 86, 91, 95, 97, 100, 120. Read one tonight.

YOU'RE NOT GOING CRAZY

I had many strange dreams after Tommy died. I vividly remember one dream in particular. In the dream, the hospital telephoned us. They had found a crying baby in the basement. The baby was Tommy and he, miraculously, had awakened. The hospital wanted us to take him home. When I awoke, I realized I was having a nightmare.

After the dream, I was standing over the bathroom sink brushing my teeth and praying—praying for strength to get through the morning. I ignored the dream because I realized it was only a cleansing dream, a flushing dream, meant to wash away the sting of death.

I want you to know that you are not going crazy just because of a few bizarre things. If you hang onto the Lord and onto faith, hope, and love, you're not going to be crazy ten years from now. Hold the Lord in one hand and sorrow in the other. Let the tears come. Let people love you and console you. Ask the Lord to wash over you and wash away all your pain. He will; I promise.

You will make it. I did, and you will too. Aren't you relieved to know that you are not going crazy? Find a way to celebrate that! Buy something, make something, or post something! Write this on a poster and put it in your kitchen. "I would have despaired unless I had believed that I would see the goodness of the Lord in the land of the living" (Psalm 27:13 NASB).

Say this "Prayer of a Lamb" out loud. In your mind's eye, take hold of the Good Shepherd's hand. "Dear Good Shepherd, take me in Your arms and hold me as a little lamb. Hold me close and don't let me go. Don't let me succumb to my dark moments, and don't let my family out of Your sight! Teach me Your ways, and lead my family and me on the level path that You have laid out for us. Blow through my spirit, soul, and body, and remove all the fog. Wash my mind of any doubt and confusion. Fill me with Your hope, strength, and courage. If You are with me, I can make it."

SPECIAL FAVORS

One day, I was trying to make a return without my receipt, and the lady wouldn't accept my return. I was furious beyond description. I've got to live without my child every day, and she's demanding something as insignificant as a silly receipt! I wanted a special favor, a special allowance, but if I had gotten it, I would have become an insufferable little monster. You and I don't want special favors because they'd become a crutch. This would lead us down a slippery slope of self pity which would produce selfishness and a slow withering-away of all we hold dear.

Rules are rules. Even life's daily routine is put in place for a reason. The daily job of fixing three meals, doing the dishes, bathing, drinking water, and taking vitamins can be our Father's way of keeping us plugged in to the world. It feels like the nuisances are killing us, but actually they are giving us life. The chores are meant to keep us alive and connected to the world.

List all the nuisances that you hate. Now give them to your Good Shepherd and ask Him to give you His strength to do them with grace, with joy, and without complaint. This is a long process. If you do the things you hate with grace, over time, the Master Sculptor will fashion you into a beautiful work of art that everyone will enjoy, including yourself.

When we choose to respond to life's little nuisances with kindness, it puts us on a path that is higher, holier, and healthier.

IS IT OK TO ASK WHY?

I believe it is ok to ask why. Something gigantic and terrible happened when our children left us. The Good Shepherd will not waste our pain. In fact, He will make one million wonderful blessings come out of our pain and out of our children's lives. God said, "Ask, and it will be given to you; seek, and you will find; knock, and it will be opened to you. For everyone who asks receives, and he who seeks finds, and to him who knocks it will be opened" (Matthew 7:7-8).

In Jeremiah 33:3, He says, "Call to Me and I will answer you, and I will tell you great and mighty things, which you do not know" (NASB). It doesn't say, "Ask Me, and I will get mad at you or shame you." No! It says He will share with us great and unsearchable things that we don't know if we just ask.

When Tommy was born, I got to hold him for twenty seconds. Then he was whisked away in order to keep him alive. I was alone in my hospital room #333 and I immediately thought of Jeremiah 33:3. I believe this was God's quirky way of communicating with me by using numbers to speak from His Book. (Do you remember the TV show "Room 222" with Karen Valentine? Then we are soul sisters!)

One year later, I was wrestling with the idea of asking God why. "Can I ask You why? Are You ok with that? Is it a lack of faith?" Then my seven-year-old came in for breakfast. She was glowing, and I immediately knew there was something different about her.

Without a word from me, she announced, "Oh Mommy, I had the most wonderful dream. Daddy, Jesus, Tommy, and I were sitting in a beautiful meadow at our farm. We were sitting at a beautiful table with meat on it. One plate had one stack of very salty meat with twenty-one pieces. Those were the questions. The other plate had three rows of meat with twenty-one pieces on each row. That meat was very peppery and those were the answers!"

The question plate is tasty and salty. The answer plate is very tasty and spicy and has three times the amount of meat. There are more answers than questions. My Father has more answers than I have questions! I felt my Father was encouraging me to go ahead and ask away!

Get this! Julie told me, "Mommy, the meat was so salty that I could actually taste it! In fact, I can still taste it now!" and she started to smack her lips. What a wonderful Father I have to speak in such a creative manner that caused me to both laugh and bow in worship to Him.

Do you have dreams about heaven? God wants you to examine the good dreams and delete the bad dreams. Do you dream about a wonderful man? The next time, see this man as a metaphor for you and the Good Shepherd; the Great Shepherd is taking you on a journey and He might use dream symbolism to speak to you. Dream interpretation books by Kevin J. Conner and Ira Mulligan have been tremendously helpful to me.

Ask God to give your children a comforting dream, just like Julie got.

JUST THE MENTION OF HIS NAME

I know it hurts to hear your child's name. I know it's a stab in the heart. I know it knocks the air out of you. I know how easy it would be to politely ask your friends and co-workers to never mention your child's name again. From what I've seen, don't do that. The healthiest women I know allow their child's name to be spoken and talked about especially by their family. This child wasn't just your child; he or she belonged to a grandmother, an aunt, a brother, or a sister. We don't want to extinguish the names of our children just because it hurts.

It is a wise woman who ignores the pain in her heart because she knows it is only temporary. She likens the name of her child to the hope of healing. She believes that the more the name is spoken, the more healing is allowed to happen to her heart. Somehow the momentary pain promotes the overall and lasting healing of the mother. I know it feels like you're going to die, but, in reality, the pain is bringing you life. I'll tell you a secret. The stabbing pain is not a knife going into your heart; it's a surgeon's needle stitching your heart. The pain you are feeling isn't hurting you; it is helping you. The more you hear your child's name, the more stitches are allowed to close the gaping hole in your heart. Just the mention of Tommy's name brings singing to my soul and hope to my heart.

I collected little Tommy dolls by Mattel. We watched every episode of the cartoon Rugrats with baby Tommy. What can you do to see or hear your child's name? Make a night shirt with their name painted on it, or make a pillowcase out of their old shirts and lay your head on their "heart."

IF YOU MISCARRIED

My friend Sophie and I don't like the word "miscarriage." It sounds so sterile and medical. We call miscarriages "heavenly adoptions" because the baby is alive in heaven, having a glorious time! So if you miscarried, think of it as your baby being heavenly adopted. Go ahead and name your baby. Go with your gut, and give your baby a boy or girl name. Your baby is still alive; except he or she is now in heaven. You will be reunited with your child one day. If you and your husband couldn't agree on a name, now is your chance to pick a name that you love, and your husband isn't crazy about! You can give your baby the longest name in history.

A week before I miscarried, I heard the Lord clearly say, "I decide life and death." I responded, "Yes Sir, I know." Little did I know, our baby, Lydia Ann, would be in the Golden City the next week. She and Tommy are playing together. If you miscarried your child, our children are rolling down hills of wildflowers where the flowers never get crushed. My daughter Julie says, "The day you die becomes your birthday in heaven." Mercy Lynn said,

"Martyrs for God get to live on the same street in heaven; it is a special honor to be on Martyrs' Row." It's like 5th Avenue or Rodeo Drive but **better**.

Who would you like your child to meet in heaven? Ask God to introduce them. As I write this today, it is President's Day, so I am asking God to introduce Tommy and his cousin Cameron, to Abraham Lincoln and George Washington!

HEAVEN'S HALL OF FAME OF FAITH

There is an ancient passage that lists the spiritual heroes and heroines. I call it the Hall of Fame of Faith. I love that the Good Shepherd lists women as well as men. Let's have a look; get God's Book, the Bible. If you don't have a Bible, buy one online. Selecting a Bible is as elaborate as buying a pair of jeans; there are so many. I think you will like the New American Standard Bible version. Get one in your favorite color. Mine is purple, and my sister Debbie has a teal one.

Anyway, let's go to the Table of Contents and find Hebrews. In Chapter 11, it says that by faith Noah, Abraham, Sarah, Moses, Rahab (the prostitute who became the great...grandmother of our Lord) and others conquered kingdoms, performed acts of righteousness, and obtained promises.

Hebrews 11:35-40 (NASB) says, "...others were tortured...others experienced mockings and scourgings, yes, also, chains and imprisonment. They were stoned; they were sawn in two; they were tempted; they were put to death with the sword; they went about...destitute, afflicted, and ill-treated...men [and women] of whom the world was not worthy... And all these, having gained approval through their faith, **did not receive what was promised** because God had provided something better for us, so that apart from us they would not be made perfect" (emphasis and brackets mine).

Skip to Hebrews 11:41. Go ahead look it up! No, I didn't make a mistake. There isn't a verse 41 "officially," but I want you to write your family's name next to verse 41. It isn't blasphemous. Lightning isn't going to strike you dead. Your signature is your statement of your faith, testifying that your God is using your family to conquer kingdoms, perform acts of righteousness, and obtain promises. Just like John Hancock before you, believe that something GOOD is about to be birthed out of your pain.

Did you receive what was promised? No. Then you are in heaven's Hall of Fame of Faith. Was your loved one sick and destitute, afflicted or ill treated? Rest assured that they are famous in heaven. Suffering for God is like winning an Oscar only a lot better. Your reward will be great. There is a city named after your child in heaven; there is a town named after your family in the Golden City. I know. You don't want a named city; you just want your loved one in your home again! You want to eat with them, and watch them as they sleep. You want to throw them a ball or talk to them.

We can try looking at their situations through their perspectives. Maybe where they are is so good and glorious that they don't want to come home. Maybe they ARE home and they are waiting for your time. (Don't try to manipulate your time; that will only sour the wine.) It's ok to miss them and to cry, but we can remind ourselves in the midst of our tears that they are having the time of their lives! They were created for the heavenly life. They are going to secret and hidden places, deep in the kingdom of heaven because of their suffering.

One day, when the time is perfect, you will join them. Until that time, make yourself ready. The more you are humble and joyful, the more places you can go in heaven. I believe those that were in a wheelchair on earth will be able to go places in heaven that will take us 10,000 years to accomplish. Ask the God of heaven to show you what your child is doing; close your eyes and wait for a picture. Don't rush the picture. Just wait, or go about your day and the picture might come later as a surprise. Don't forget to write your family's name next to verse 41.

A SHIELD OF FAITH

Let me tell you what happened the night my friend Dawn and I visited Sophie. I mentioned Sophie in Chapter 15. She learned that her baby, John Raul, died in utero when she was 32 weeks along. Sophie had to go through the pain and contractions of labor in the middle of the night, and not end up with a baby that was alive. Sophie said she wanted to be alone, but I had been in this situation and knew it was a nightmare. I never wanted someone to repeat it alone. I decided I would go to the hospital with Dawn, my best friend, and wait in the waiting room. If Sophie changed her mind, we would be there.

Dawn became one of my best friends because she helped me get out of bed after Tommy died. Her little Bradley went to heaven several years before Tommy and she was a forerunner for me to follow. Dawn is a powerhouse. I learned a lot from her. The compassion that Dawn showed me I was able to share with Sophie. With this book, I am reaching out to you so that in years to come, you can reach out to someone you know.

As Dawn and I waited in the lobby, she rehearsed things we needed to do when we saw Sophie. First, we asked God to fill us with His strength, power, and love. Second, we would tell her how beautiful her baby looked. All mothers want to hear that their babies are beautiful. And third, we were going to take some photos. If she wanted them later, she would have them. The three of us were reunited in Sophie's hospital room. Her sweet husband was there as well. This is one of my most precious memories.

A week after our hospital visit, Sophie's husband called our house and asked to speak to my husband. Being a good follower of Lucille Ball, I listened in on the other phone! Here is the story in his words. "On the night that Dawn and Nancy walked into the hospital, I saw they were carrying something bright and shiny; in fact, it was glowing. I rubbed my eyes several times, and saw that they were carrying gold shields that were covered in jewels. They each had a shield and there was something written on the shields, but the Lord was not letting me read it. I think what they were carrying were Shields of Faith. They brought faith, hope, and love when we had none. They protected us when we were going through the darkest time of our life. I want to thank Nancy for coming. If they hadn't come, we might have spiraled down to the pit of despair and never returned."

I hope this book is your Shield of Faith. I hope you use the prayers and prescriptions in each chapter (and at the back of this book) for yourself. Try to only read one a day. Let the words marinate in your soul. I hope that one day you will reach out and help others. You can start now if you want. Find someone you can encourage today and be their Shield of Faith even if you feel weak with little faith. A hug goes a long way. Buy extra copies of this book and share the with those who need it. Leave it in a restaurant bathroom. Be an angel for someone else.

THE GRAVESTONE

Sophie asked me if I went to see Tommy's gravestone right away. I suppose if Tommy's grave was closer, I would visit more often. To be honest, I have only been there three times. It is depressing for me to visit. On the other hand, I feel his presence more strongly when I go.

It's vague to me now. The first time we visited the site, they were digging the hole for another child; that part I remember vividly. I lay across Tommy's little piece of grass and wailed and wailed. We had our kids with us. I am a crier, so it didn't really bother them to see me cry. I'm sure they thought, "There goes Mommy again, doing what she does best!"

I think it is healthy for children to see their parents cry in these situations. It shows them that we would cry for them if they were gone. It shows them they can cry if they want to. My crying showed my children that I cried and lived! Later, we went out to dinner and I was my normal self. I always reassure them, "I am crying, but I will be fine."

Of course, when I visit, I talk to him. Before I lost a child, I use to think that was weird. Now, unfortunately, I understand. My pastor told me I might want to talk at the gravesite and I am glad that he told me so.

I hope it is encouraging to you that the gravesite scenes are very vague to me now. My reaction today will become your reaction tomorrow. The sad situation today will soon be a vague memory tomorrow. You feel rotten today, but later you will be able to laugh, hum, and stroll through a park without being sad. Hold sorrow in one hand and the Lord in the other, and you will make it. I promise.

If you don't have a gravesite or if it's across the ocean in another country, you can pick a special park and make that your resting place. I wouldn't set up a tombstone in your backyard. I think that would enshrine your child and ensnare you. You can have a little garden in remembrance of your child. What if you plant sunflowers to remember your little sweetheart! Sunflowers will remind you of your child's smiling face and that he or she is so happy in heaven.

SUFFERING

I am going to take a stab at why there are people who suffer with illnesses. I haven't read anything that suggests what I'm about to suggest, but I think it will ring true in your spirit.

It is not blasphemous to question God about suffering. I approach any subject from the perspective that my Daddy God in Heaven is a good daddy. If something happened that's not good, there MUST be a logical explanation. I am giving it a Godly spin. Why did a loved one suffer through an illness? A friend of mine, Lizabeth, recently died at the hospital. I asked my Father why this happened.

"Nancy, I don't want anyone to be sick. I don't make anyone sick to 'teach them a lesson.' Sickness is part of your world. I make all bad things work together for good for those who love me." (See Romans 8:28.) "Therefore we do not lose heart, but though our outer man is decaying, yet our inner man is being renewed day by day....producing for us an eternal weight of glory far beyond all comparison" (2 Corinthians 4:16 NASB). We see sick people, but our Father sees muscle men and wonder women. As they get sicker and sicker on earth, they are getting stronger and stronger in the spirit, and they are producing for themselves eternal rewards beyond our wildest comprehension.

Don't focus on the pain they felt on earth because in an instant, when someone enters heaven, all the pain drifts away. The pain is evaporated and is only a vague memory like a hazy dream we can't grasp.

Lastly, I believe that the more we suffer or the more we serve others, the more our eternal weight will be in heaven. I believe that blind people will be able to see things in heaven that others cannot. I believe that those that are bound to a wheelchair today will go to new heights in heaven that others will have to be trained to do. I believe that those in the Rwanda genocide live on the Martyr's Circle in heaven, and now they are kings and queens.

I don't know about you, but I'm not letting the phrase "beyond comprehension" stop me from trying to imagine. Make a list of weights of glory in the margin of this book that you want for you and your family. God gave me a dream that my friend Lizabeth had a huge opera symphony house named after her because of her faith. It was larger than any Super Bowl coliseum! What rewards does your child have? Think of tangible things. Let your imagination run wild. Make a list here.

STAY ALIVE

L isten to the stern words spoken by Daniel Day Lewis from the movie, *Last of the Mohicans*: "You stay alive! Be strong! Survive! Stay alive, no matter what occurs! I **will** find you. No matter how long it takes, no matter how far. I will find you." The hero, Hawkeye, must leave his bride in the hands of the enemy. With his face set like flint, he begged his new bride to stay alive. As he implored her to live, it reminded me of my situation. Like the taste of blood in my mouth, I could taste the sting of death. The sound of aching pain was ringing in my ears. All I could see was my pain.

Now, through Hawkeye's eyes, I could see how God felt about me! He was so earnest about me staying alive. He was passionate for me and for life! I remember feeling the yearning of His heart inside of my heart. **"Stay alive!"** It echoed inside of my soul. He wanted me to live because He had so much He wanted to give to me in this life on earth. He didn't want our story to end. He wanted to find me and put my shattered heart back together so that we could have a beautiful life together now on earth.

When I wanted to let go, I reached up to Him. He caught me and pulled me out of the mire. He found me and cut off the fetters that were around my neck and ankles. When I didn't think that I could go on, I called for help and He came running. He carried me to a high mountain so that I could see the marvelous future we had together. Our future had a destiny. I had only to wait and trust. When I hurt, He hurt. When I hurt, He heard. When I hurt, He healed.

The Good Shepherd says to you, "You stay alive! Be strong! Survive! Stay alive, no matter what occurs! I am with you. No matter how long it takes, no matter how far you go, I am with you!" He has a beautiful life that He wants to give you here on earth.

If you like movies, check out *Ever After* with Drew Barrymore. It will inspire you to stay alive, be strong and survive—no matter what. *The Last of the Mohicans* has strong, graphic content that might not be your preference. Maybe your husband could watch it and pause it for you when the "Stay alive! Survive!" speech comes on.

DISHING IT OUT

I found out I had a lot of buried anger after Tommy died. I don't think losing Tommy was the only event that made me that angry. I think God saw it all the time and the pain was like heat under a kettle of gold—the dross and impurities came out.

In the beginning of this process, I was a baby. I ranted and raved at God on a regular basis. I figured God could handle it. But as I matured, I realized God didn't deserve that kind of treatment, so I stopped. It took ten years for me to get to that place though. We love our teenage daughters, but do we really deserve their diva demands? Heck no!

One day, I told God, "Crap! Crap! Crap! That is all You ever dish out, and then You expect me to dig through it and look for diamonds! Well, I am not going to do it anymore." God doesn't change. He is the great I Am. He didn't yell back, but He did stay silent. I decided I didn't want to go another day without Him. Gradually, taking baby steps toward Him and His ways, I was led to diamonds in the rough. In fact, I became the diamond that God was sculpting. YOU are the diamond that God is sculpting now. You are God's little treasure chest of jewels. (See Isaiah 54:11-13.)

Go out today and buy a ring that won't turn your finger blue. Buy whatever you can afford: Wal-Mart or Tiffany's. Splurge on a gift for yourself, but let it remind you that you are God's little ruby. And even though we feel yuck, it is temporary. I promise if you draw near to God, He will draw near to you, and He will put the sparkle back in your life.

Day 22

DON'T GIVE ME THAT CRAP

I told you I had a lot of anger issues during that time in my life. One day, when I was in deep depression, I "heard" or felt a nudge from God trying to console me. The conversation went something like this: "Nancy I know you are really sad right now, and I can't explain everything to you; all I can do is promise that I will make it up to you. You have My Word." In my very mature response to Him, I retorted, "Don't give that 'I'll make it up to you' crap! There is no way You can make it up to me."

I continued my ranting, "My son is not here. Jeremiah doesn't have his brother. There is a hole in the minivan and a bigger hole in my heart! He will never get to wear those cute little baby outfits. He will never wear the 'First Christmas' PJs. And each birthday is a sad reminder that another year rolled around and he is not here. How can You make it up to me if I am going to spend my life without him?"

But that is just it. I won't spend my entire life without him—only forty years. I will have 1000 million years with him and more.

Do you see how small forty years is compared to eternity? One day, sorrow will melt away like a dream I can't remember. And I now know that God will make it up to me; He will have 100 million years to do it! Tommy and I will be walking through fields of flowers that never get crushed, flying through other galaxies, and running through waves of crystal-blue water with no stinging jellyfish!

Have you allowed yourself to voice your anger at God? I know a lady that was so mad at God that she "saw" herself throwing dynamite at Him. It blew up on Him. He was burned and charred but when the smoke cleared, He, the Good Shepherd, still had eyes of forgiveness and compassion. Now that's love! It's dangerous to stay angry at God. End your ranting by saying something positive about God.

Let me help you with this Anger Prayer: "Dear God, I am so fighting mad at You! I didn't even get to _____ with my child! I was planning to _____ with them! Now I'll never get to _____ with them. Nevertheless, You hold the words of eternal life and there is no one like You. I don't want to live alone, slugging through life. I choose to believe that You love me and will explain everything when I see You. In the meantime, I am looking forward to _____ with my child in heaven."

Get a notebook and keep a running list of all the things that you will do with your child when you are face to face. One thing I am planning to do is skip across the stars, as one jumps across stones in a pond, while holding Tommy's hand.

LIFE SUPPORT

While we were going through our trauma, we had a lot of support. We had meals brought every day. I had rides to the hospital. My friends babysat my kids. I had visitors at the hospital practically every day. Before Tommy arrived, our community was young, busy, and self-centered. We took care of our families, but that was about it. A year before Tommy was born, my prayer for my community was for us to become "space invaders." I wanted us to press into other people's lives. It seemed we were too busy to care about anything beyond the kitchen sink.

One lady claimed Tommy had become the catalyst that melted the thick veneer off our lives. In the end, our community became a beautiful symphony of love. In fact, Julie, my seven-year-old, said that when Tommy died, the church became our life support. They held, hugged, and loved us as we were—broken and miserable. They lived and breathed for us when we didn't have the strength. They became our tendons when we couldn't move. They became the Neosporin in our infected wounds. They valued us above themselves; not looking to their own interests but to the interests of our family. (See Philippians 2:4.)

I want that same kind of support for you. There were several times at church that I fell apart and lay in a pile on the floor. No one looked down on me or quoted some stupid cliché. What I'm trying to say is that it is easier to stay home, but you will miss out on quicker healing. Go wearing waterproof mascara, and let the music wash away the hurt and confusion. Let people hug you. I believe that hugs have a supernatural healing power from God. You may cry, and that's ok. Whoever is chosen for your tears on their shoulder is an angel and won't mind being there for you.

If you don't have "life support," google *House of Prayer* on the internet. You might find that God talks straight to your heart in the atmosphere of prayer and worship. Be relentless. Find a place that will be your hands and feet and will hold your heart next to theirs.

A BRIEF LIFE IS NOT AN INCOMPLETE LIFE

Tommy changed our selfishness, but he was only a baby who lived for three and a half months; he never spoke a word or took a step, but he lived a **full** life. He never showed his pain, but he made us, the community, realize that our lives were painfully out of balance. His heart was deformed, but maybe it was our hearts that were broken. He was confined to a bed, yet he did more good in his little bed than we do in our walking lives. We thought we had a good life. In reality, it was a masquerade. We looked good on the outside, but we didn't have anything underneath.

He helped us take off our masks and get real. What about your child? How did he change and challenge people? How did his laughter and joy for life encourage people? God completed His destiny in our children's lives even though they had shorter lives. My sister-in-law Suzie says that a brief life is not an incomplete life.

Think about how your child's life affected others positively. Even if it was a very short life, can you see that it was full?

Read the cards that people gave you. Put them in a special box or in a scrapbook. Read one card every week. Write them a thank you if their card touched your heart. And if you send a sympathy card, **please** write something personal. It doesn't have to be long or lofty. Your words are water to a parched soul.

DOING WHAT YOU DREAD

In every journey of healing, there comes a time when we must cross a rickety bridge. The name of that bridge is "Dread." We are afraid that if we walk across it, we will fall through a rotten piece of lumber into an icy creek. By avoiding our dreads, we are already in the dark pit. Dread robs us of our future by keeping us bound to past pain. Freedom and joy live on the other side of dread. Overcoming my dreads became my life support.

Last night, I watched the movie *John Q* starring Denzel Washington. It is a movie about a sick little boy in a hospital. For weeks at the video store, I felt the Lord's whisper suggesting that I watch it. My answer was what it always was: "Next week, Lord." That lasted for 250 weeks! Well, last night, the movie was on TV. I squeezed my Father's hand while I watched it. What healing! I felt so empowered for doing what I dreaded! It wasn't as "dreadful" as I thought. My husband even came in by "accident," and he watched it too. What a sweet release.

Other areas of dread were my fears of returning to Tommy's hospital and of going to a baby shower. The dark and dreary hospital parking garage was the **worst**! It felt like I was walking in an active volcano. I forced myself to walk through it. I found that fear didn't have a hold on me anymore. It was probably two or more years before I went to a baby shower. Give yourself some time to heal, but don't avoid those events forever.

Remember, you don't have to do them alone. The Good Shepherd is waiting to hold your hand and brush back your hair as you take a deep breath and move forward. I promise that the promises you crave lie on the other side of your dread. I love you so much. Ask the Good Shepherd to help you believe in yourself in the same way that He believes in you. Step out and overcome a dread by holding Him in one hand and what you dread in the other.

Try this prayer against dread: "I am so weak that I don't think I can even tie my own shoes. Give me Your strength for the small daily things. There are so many things that I dread! Inject into my heart Your courage. Give me Your grace and peace so that I don't have to rush into everything related to life. I am so scared, Lord. Fill the void that is in my heart without _____ with Your perfect, divine love. (Be still and wait for Him to fill you.) Fill... Fill... Fill... Touch my family the way You're touching me. Heal us spirit, soul, and body."

DON'T PULL THE PLUG ON GOD

After a heart-wrenching experience, it is easy to pull the plug on God. But He is madly and crazily in love with you and your family. He is not your enemy. Stay connected to Him. Let Him nurse and caress your heart back to life. Let Him be your source of strength and nutrients. I know we can live without God, but I don't think we can be **alive** without God.

On Valentine's Day, Tommy died; he was not raised from the dead as we had believed he would be. The miracle is that I was raised from the dead! I know my God is the resurrection and the life because He raised me up. I was a woman who was afraid of the dark. I was an over-protective mother in every sense of the word. Everyone who knew me was worried about me. If they're honest, they'll tell you they didn't think I would make it.

But I had a truth deep in my heart that kept me alive. I knew that if I stayed plugged into God, He would take care of everything. I knew that my life was not dependent on fate but on my Father in heaven. I knew if I stayed connected to faith and not fate, I would be all right. I knew if I kept holding His hand, the Good Shepherd would bring me through the fire. I knew if I climbed on His shoulders, He'd bring me through the flood.

I was so disappointed when Tommy died; make no mistake about it. But I was not going to give up on God, who is the best thing in my life, just because I didn't get what I hoped for. I had to confess my anger at God and "forgive" Him. I had to be honest about my pain and give the issues to God so that He could wash them away.

Have you allowed yourself to voice your anger at God? Your anger can't hold a candle to His Love. Hold the Good Shepherd's hand and look Him in the eye. Say this "Trusting Him Brings Vision" prayer out loud: "How could You let this happen? You are supposed to protect us. Where were You? Heavenly Father, I am so confused and angry. I know I can't hold this in, or I will explode. So clean me out God. I release all today's anger and bitterness to You. (Breathe out.) Take it all. I don't want it. (Try to imagine today's anger evaporating away.) I don't like **what** happened, but I am going to trust that You will work the bad situation into good. Give me eyes to see, ears to hear, and a heart to perceive that You are with me and that I am not walking alone. Open my ears to hear Your still, small, sweet voice. Open my mouth to speak the truth in love. Open my eyes to see Your path that You have set out for me. Help me to perceive Your ways."

EVERY MOVEMENT

Every significant movement begins with a martyr. I believe Martin Luther King Jr. was a modern day martyr for our country. I believe God sovereignly used Dr. King's life and death as the catalyst for the Civil Rights movement. Unless a seed dies, it can never produce fruit. Martin Luther King, Jr. was the seed that died to produce the fruit of civil rights for all. I even believe that Reverend King knew he was going to die for this cause. I believe our Father asked for Martin's permission to take his life and use it.

Tommy was on life support from the moment he took his first breath. He hung between two worlds for too long. Then one day, I had this thought that maybe Tommy was hanging in between life and death because God was waiting for me to give Him permission to take Tommy. My mature response was, "Well, if You're waiting for me to give You permission to take Tommy's life, I will under one condition: **after hell freezes over!**" I have a very honest and real relationship with God. I figure He already sees the ugliness in my heart, so I might as well get it out on the table for me to examine.

"I assure you, most solemnly I tell you, if a grain of wheat falls into the earth and dies… it produces many others and yields a rich harvest" (John 12:24 AMP). I'll bet your child had a selfless heart. Those are the kinds of hearts God uses to change the world. When a selfless heart dies, it produces a huge harvest. Just as Martin Luther King Jr. had to die to change the world, so it is with your child.

The Good Shepherd didn't take your child; the circumstances of a broken world did. The Good Shepherd didn't "need" your child in heaven! But He is going to take this terrible tragedy and turn it around, using your child as a forerunner of a movement that is going to change your community. I don't know how, but I **know** this fact by faith. Our Heavenly Father takes the smallest people and makes them into heroes. You don't even have to champion a cause for them. I believe our Father will do it for you. He is using the life and death of your child to wrestle people's hearts back to Him. I know it is weird and seems unfair that your heart is being wrenched while others are being expanded, but not to worry. Your prize will be revealed in due time.

Aren't you amazed that the Good Shepherd would use your child in the same way He used Martin Luther King Jr.?

Here's the balance. Don't let this idea go to your head, or it will lead to enshrinement. You will enshrine yourself and your child. Idolatry is ugly. The safety net of this idea is to hold it loosely. In fact, don't hang on to it at all. Give it back to your Father God in heaven. On one side of your mouth praise God for your loved one who was a champion, but on the other side, say to your Father, "Take this situation and use it. I submit to Your will. Thank You for using my family and for using me."

LONG DISTANCE TO HEAVEN

I wish we could talk to our kids (or loved ones) in heaven even if it was only once a year. I just want to hear Tommy's voice and find out what he has been doing.

Because Tommy was on a ventilator, I never heard Tommy's voice, not even a cry. I don't even know what toys he would prefer over others. My curiosity used to send me into orbit! I kept begging and begging for a dream about Tommy in heaven, but all I got was silence. I decided to trust the Good Shepherd's silence. Since He had revealed a lot of truths to me but now He was silent, I finally had to trust that my heavenly Father knew best. I asked Him to take away my curiosity.

A long time later, my friend Vicky told me something she thought was silly. I thought it was a dream come true. "Nancy, did you know my son has always wanted to be called Tommy James? When he was a little boy, he announced to us that his new name was 'Tommy James' but we could call him T.J. for short!"

Wow! My Father was showing me something about my son. I could look at her son to get a tiny glimpse of the personality of my son. I believe her son had some similarities that I could admire and imagine were a part of my son's life.

I know God will leave you little bread crumbs that will give you hints about your child. It's ok to dream and imagine what your child is doing. You can't talk to him or her, but you can tell God to give your child a message from you. My daughter, Mercy would paint pictures and ask God to take a photograph of it to show Tommy. Wow! From then on, I had my kids draw, paint, or build Legos and then I asked God to show their creations to Tommy.

Share this idea with your kids today. It will bring them so much peace that God can record family milestones such as football games, weddings, graduations, or Dad surfing and show them to their sibling (and a million of their closest relatives) in heaven. God might even set up a big screen TV in heaven and watch the game live! When I say **big** screen, I mean a mile-long screen!

MARTHA'S FAITH

Several weeks after we said goodbye to Tommy, I was given an incredible "divine download of truth." I was driving into downtown, and just as I was coming to the McKinney Avenue exit, the Good Shepherd said to me, "Some televangelists teach that it takes **great** faith for a miracle. Baloney! It only takes a mustard seed of faith for a miracle. I say, what you are walking in, is **greater** faith than even you can imagine. You still have faith in Me and miracles, even though you didn't get the one thing you really wanted. Now **that** is great faith!" (See Matthew 17:20.) I got the impression that sometimes human faith is loud, proud, and exhausting; Godly faith is a secret and quiet work of the heart.

There is an old story of two sisters. One sister we'll call Martha Stalwart. Martha demonstrated her faith through works: an outward show of her faith. She had every t crossed and every i dotted. She was a desperate housewife on steroids and Prozac. She was a prisoner in her own world, afraid to come out and be real. She lived in the constant fear that if she didn't carry the torch perfectly, she would get burned. She believed her life's destiny was in her hands. She could never rest because she always saw the job was never done.

Her sister, Mary, on the other hand, was quite the opposite. Mary was more of a free spirit; she let the important things of life take center stage instead of herself. She had a childlike heart and was able to trust God to balance the scales. She kept her eyes on the heavenly prize instead of on the earthly trials. She knew good would come, but so would the bad. She didn't blame herself or her husband for her troubles. She knew the bad would pass in time. She knew her life's destiny was not in her own hands. She rested in the knowledge of trusting her Father God to work all things for good. She did her best without having to meet every task with perfection.

As Jesus stayed at Martha and Mary's house, Mary was the one who sat at the Lord's feet, listening to what He taught. Meanwhile, Martha was distracted by the big dinner she was preparing. She came to Jesus and said, "Lord, isn't it unfair that my sister just sits here while I do all the work? Tell her to come and help me."

"But the Lord said to her, 'My dear Martha, you are worried and upset over all these details! There is only one thing worth being concerned about. Mary has discovered it...'" (Luke 10:41-42 NLT).

Let me relate this story to faith. When troubles come, we can work, pray, fast, shake that tambourine, rub those crystals, or meditate for hours on end, hoping to obtain our miracles through works on our part. Basically, Martha lived in a constant state of striving, doubting, and condemning. Or we can be like Mary; do our best and trust God to work everything out according to His mysterious plan. We can rest knowing we don't hold the whole world in our hands. We have our Father doing that impossible job.

If you believed God for a miracle and you did not receive what you hoped for, rest in this fact: you had enough faith. God is in control of life and death. There are mysterious things that cannot be explained to us on this side of heaven. Trust Him that He is good, kind, and faithful. Don't blame God or yourself.

Take some time out of your day and get alone with the Good Shepherd. I think we are all a little like Martha, and we need to be a little more like Mary. Take His hand and say this prayer of "Exchanging His Love for Fear" out loud: "Lord, disconnect me from all fear that makes me live in a constant state of performance and perfection. Take me off the treadmill. Wrap Yourself around me, and infuse into every cell of my spirit, soul, and body that I am accepted by You, my Heavenly Daddy. Make me have a Mary heart. Reveal to me that being loved and mesmerized by You is the only really important thing that matters. Show me how to change my habits and to walk in Your ways of joy and peace."

BUDDY AND SPARKY

As I write to you, my two dogs sit between my legs. They usually jockey for position and fight for the right to sit the closest to me. I marvel at their love for me. They are helpless without me. Sometimes, I have to be away from my dogs for a whole day. That must seem like an eternity to my dogs. It breaks my heart! I wish I could explain to them why I must leave and that I'll return. When I return, they ask no questions; they merely jump into my arms and plant a bunch of sloppy kisses all over my face. Then it's business as usual. They act as if nothing happened. They don't even so much as pout. WOW!

The dogs and I are not equals. I am their master and that will never change. But neither will my love ever change for them. No matter how many times they pee on my furniture, I love them (eventually). If I can love my dogs unconditionally, how much **more** can God love me?

I can learn a lot from my dogs in regard to my relationship with God. God, my Heavenly Father, provides everything I need for life. I love to sit close to Him. I love to read His stories and hear His voice. When He calls my name, it is life to me.

Sometimes, it seems like my Heavenly Father has to go away for a while. It seems like an eternity. My pride and insecurity gets a little hurt. I understand He isn't very far away from anyone. All we must do is call His name, and He comes running. It breaks His heart when we hurt. I know He's dying to explain His actions, but He can't explain eternity to finite minds at this time. I have learned that I can't run away from my Master just because I feel hurt. I have to remember all the good times we've had together. I love Him too much, and He loves me. If I ran away, to whom would I run? Who could truly love me, flaws and all, the way He does?

I believe that everything my Heavenly Father does will be explained to me one day. Until that time, I am going to sit in His lap and follow His voice when He calls.

Whose voice are you listening to? God's true voice is still, small, and sweet. If you hear anything else, **hang up!** Take His hand and say this prayer: "Lord, take the new sorrows and restlessness in my heart and replace them with Your contentment and peace. Help me to hear Your voice that is still, small, and sweet. I want to hear You say my name. Make me like Mary, and help me to be looking up to You and not at my troubles. Replace any worries I have with Your faith."

Day 31

OUR FATHER: THE PRODUCER AND DIRECTOR

I love to listen to a director's commentary about a movie he has made. I know there are only six people on the planet who share my vice, but I devour a movie's commentary especially if the director explains not only the technical merits but also divulges the symbolism as well. I watch the movie commentary because I want to learn from the director. I learn why he took the movie one way or why he was silent in another. The director's ways are mysterious and creative. Many times there were several choices put before him, but he makes his decision based on the direction he wants the story to go.

I believe our Heavenly Father is the Great Director behind the movie called "Our Life." We are the screenwriters because He gives us freewill. He allows us to call the shots. We are wise to ask His counsel and direction.

"I will bless the Lord who has counseled me; indeed, my mind instructs me in the night. I have set the Lord continually before me; because He is at my right hand, I will not be shaken. Therefore my heart is glad and my glory rejoices…You will make known to me the path of life; in Your presence is fullness of joy; in Your right hand there are pleasures forever" (Psalm 16:7-9,11 NASB).

Most of the time, there is no such thing as a wrong move because the Great Director will just re-calculate—much like the maps on our smart phones! Rarely will He step in unless it is mandatory to keep our life decisions from tipping the delicate balance of all of mankind. God told me a week before Tommy died, "Nancy, I know you want Me to feel sorry for you and just let your son live. 'What difference will one little boy make?' you say. But I say to you, that if I let one decision happen apart from My perfect will, then the earth will fall off its axis, and I am not going to let that happen." (Holy mackerel! He really **does** hold the whole world in His hands!) "If I let Tommy live, then everyone who prayed for Him will have their lives ruined. Everyone that was connected to Tommy in some way or another will have ravaged lives." (It would be the reverse of the movie *It's a Wonderful Life*.) "They will think that healing comes after they jump through a million hoops. I can't let that happen."

The Great Director expects us to ask what, when, how, and why. He likes dialogue and camaraderie. If we ask, "Please help me know You better by explaining this situation to me," it puts us in the position of humility. Humility always puts us in the place of blessing. It illumines the best path forward.

LAUGHTER

Scientists have proven that laughter is the best medicine. I chuckle when science mirrors scripture. Remember the proverb, "A merry heart doeth good like a medicine" (Proverbs 17:22 KJV). Knowing this fact influenced our choice to watch comedies, chick-flicks, and anything that made us "feel good." I normally love thrillers and action movies, but after Tommy died, I wasn't able to handle anything beyond a PG. I fought this tendency by forcing myself to sit through movies like *Mission Impossible*, but my body couldn't handle the adrenalin rush caused by the action scenes. I had lived through a real life mission impossible, and it was time to rest.

It got to the point that G-rated movies were just perfect for me. I remember when this truth hit my heart. I was watching Disney's *The Kid*, and I had to accept that I was different now. I had to stop fighting the new me—go the way of peace. The fruit of peace followed G-rated movies. The new me needed rest, even in the movies I watched and in the life choices I made.

I wonder how many hearts have been helped just by watching *Seinfeld* or *Friends*?

What are your favorite television shows? Comedies are a nice prescription for momentary anesthesia. Too much anesthesia can numb us to the point where we can't really live. Too much anesthesia makes us the *walking dead*. If you watch a comedy and invite the Lord's presence, it will multiply all the good effects of the comedy and heal the deepest part of your soul. God created comedy. He made Bob Hope, Bill Cosby, Tina Fey, Steve Carroll, and all the comedians we love today. Take the time to watch or record some new comedy shows and movies.

KNOW FEAR = NO PEACE

Eight years before Tommy died, I was up late one evening, meditating and reading my Bible. I was reading David's statement, "I sought the Lord, and He answered me, and delivered me from all my fears" (Psalm 34:4 NASB). The phrase "all my fears" captured my attention. This was the same David who, as a boy, stopped a giant from destroying his people. I thought, *if he has fear problems, we're all in a lot of trouble.*

I prayed the same thing: "Deliver me from all my fears." I know about fear. I know I have a lot of fears. Talk about a laundry list! As a grown woman, I was afraid of the dark; I was even afraid to get out of my bed at night! That night, I decided I didn't want to be a slave to fear anymore. Fear is a tormentor. So I asked my Father God to get rid of the fear inside of me.

That night, I had two dreams. In the first dream, Bill Cosby was God, and he was driving a drycleaner's truck. Bill Cosby is so cute and adorable; he makes great stand-in for God! I wanted to drive his truck, but he said, "No, I've got this." When I awoke,

I had these sweet thoughts that interpreted the dream. "Nancy, sit back and rest. Let Me do the driving. I know where we are going!" We were in a drycleaner's truck to symbolize that He wanted to be my spot remover. He wanted me to stop pointing out my flaws and spots. "I like you the way you are."

In the second dream, I was afraid of my menstrual period. I was in junior high and the sight of blood sent me screaming down the hall. Talk about weird! Instead of interpreting the dream symbolically, I took it literally. I forgot that ninety percent of dreams are symbolic. As the years marched on, I had that dream quite often. I didn't take the advice of the first dream that told me to rest. Instead, I kept spinning out of control, trying to fix myself.

Later, God revealed that I had worshipped fear. "Oh God, come on! I don't worship fear." I replied. He said in a stern voice, "Oh yes, you do worship fear. You have more faith that something bad is going to happen than faith in My ability to protect you." When fear is on the throne of our hearts, it taints our minds out of sound wisdom.

What are you afraid of? Get a spiral notebook and list your fears! Then renounce each one of those fears out loud. Say: "With God's help, I renounce the fear of _____." Then keep reading, and I will show you how to live in faith. Believe it or not, it is God's perfect love that dismantles the work, power, and torment of fear.

NO FEAR = KNOW PEACE

At the end of eight years, I had a turning point concerning the dream. Tommy was our little baby who was so sick that after months of faith, fasting, and prayer, he remained at eternity's door. On February 8th, we met with our pastors to discuss our options. With our pastors' love, they supported us in our decision to take Tommy off life support. We had to do what every parent fears: make that decision. It was a very difficult decision, but God never left our side. Tom and I decided that God could either heal Tommy or take him to heaven. In fact, we felt a modern-day Bible story was being played out in our lives. Just as God provided a way for Abraham, we felt confident that God would provide a way out for us.

That night, I had a wonderfully strange dream. I sat up in bed stunned. I got out of bed and went to my knees. For the first time, the dream revealed that I was not afraid of my period. Then, I had a sweet thought in my heart. God said, "Congratulations, Nancy. You're not afraid of death anymore!" Wow! In that moment, I remembered my Shakespeare classes in high school: spilt blood always symbolized death. "I'm not afraid of death!" I rejoiced.

The Bible teaches that the number eight represents new beginnings. On February 8th, eight years after the dream was revealed, I was free! I had no fear. Praise God Almighty I was free at last.

I now believe that from the foundation of the world, God's destiny for Tommy was to live a short life. I don't think God caused Tommy's situation just to rid me of fear. God loves people even with their hang-ups. God's gift to me for going through that hell was to free me from the tyranny of fearing death. Further, I have traveled to Africa, Europe, and Central America by myself without any fear. This is another blessing that came out of my trauma.

Did you make a list of fears and renounce them, with declaration in your soul? Now, say this out loud: "Good Shepherd, I do not want to live in fear anymore. I renounce fear and all its torment over me and my family. I ask You, Lord, to remove every trace of fear from my spirit, soul, and body. Inject into every cell of my being Your power, Your love, and Your sound mind. I give You permission to dismantle the work of fear in my life. Separate me from any family tendency toward fear. Today, I set up a new foundation of faith in You."

NO FEAR FOREVER

No fear forever! I was now free from the tyranny of death. Think of the gift that I was going to be to my family. My children lost a sibling, but for some reason they don't have extraordinary fears. It would be worse for them if we lost our faith. I survived my worst nightmare and was still alive. What I thought would kill me didn't. It hurt a lot but not as much as I feared or dreaded. How did I survive? I held my Daddy's hand, and He was talking to me through the whole ordeal.

I remember the miserable, terrible, chewed-up, tied-up, wound-up little wretch I once was. I shudder when I think of my old condition. Even my husband didn't know what a shrivel-souled woman I was. I didn't know until I felt freedom and allowed my Father to take me to the high places. I felt like I had climbed Mt. Everest.

Now I'm a gorgeous, gigantic, passionate, precious, powerful woman of God. I was a slave in a dungeon; now I own the castle and the entire countryside. I possess powerful keys to the Kingdom.

I know you may not feel like much more than a chipped piece of glass, but give the Potter a spin at His wheel and He'll make you into a fine piece of china. Before you know it, you'll be a vessel that will be filled to overflowing. You will even bless others.

Fear is a tormentor. Fear is not from God. Our Good Shepherd gives us His power, His love, and His sound mind if we ask Him. If we live in fear, then we won't have God's wisdom to make right choices. God doesn't want us to live in torment.

Take that list of your fears and ask God to deliver you of **all** your fears. He will do it. It won't happen overnight, but it will happen! When it does, buy a plaque declaring your new victory over fear.

Write this on several index cards and say it out loud until you mean it: "Good Shepherd, I do not want to live in fear anymore. I renounce fear and all its torment over me and my family. I ask You, Lord, to remove every trace of fear from my spirit, soul, and body. Inject into every cell of my being, Your power, Your love, and Your sound mind. I give You permission to dismantle the work of fear in my life. Separate me from any family tendency toward fear. Today, I set up a new foundation of faith in You."

Day **36**

ALL PRAISE FOR JOB

There is an ancient hero named Job. In one day, he lost all ten of his children, all his investments, all his employees, all his houses, all his friends, and his health. I have heard it said that Job lost everything because he was a fearful person. This was demonstrated by his comment, "What I feared has come upon me." Our Good Shepherd describes Job as being blameless and upright; therefore, there was no fault or cause in Job for his suffering. We've all had a bad day or a bad decade but nothing like what Job suffered.

Why did the Good Shepherd allow Job to suffer? I believe that Job served as an object lesson for all of us. The Good Shepherd needed one person to encourage us to keep running the race set before us. He didn't want Job to suffer; rather, He allowed him to suffer for our benefit. I believe the Good Shepherd specifically picked someone who was not only blameless but could also handle the pressure of losing everything. God knew mankind would enable its own suffering: suffering that God never wanted for us. God knew we would inflict on ourselves such suffering as genocide, drunk driving, rape, and war, to name a few.

No one has lost more than Job, and somehow that knowledge helps us to bear up under the weight of our trials. God knew that the story of a blameless-yet-cursed Job would somehow give us someone with which to identify in the depths of our pain.

Our Heavenly Father went even one step further than merely giving us, in Job, a partner in pain. Job showed us that blind faith in God's inscrutable wisdom can itself help us cope with our suffering. Listen to what Job said when he lost everything: "God gives and God takes away. Blessed be the name of the Lord." Wow! That response is as good an illustration of true faith as can be found anywhere!

Fear keeps us from true love, great strength, and a sound mind. Fear is what happens when we don't trust God. I do think that if we live in fear, if fear is on the throne of our hearts, fear can be a magnet for destruction. God doesn't bring trouble on us as punishment for not trusting Him. Our Heavenly Father is not persuaded to be vengeful or impatient. He is very compassionate and merciful, and He knows we are just kids made out of dirt.

I was a weak and very fearful person, but I kept seeking God for help. If you've had angry and hateful thoughts toward God, don't beat yourself up. Your Father understands anger comes out of fear. He knows you are hurting, and hurting people hurt other people. Don't stay mad at God. Ask Him to forgive you and to cleanse your heart with a good bar of soap! God is all-wise and all-knowing. He has your back. If He gave His own Son for us, how will He not freely give us all the things we need?

It's understandable that after this trauma you feel unsafe for yourself and your children. Trusting God is your only hope. A person finds life by trusting God; it disconnects us from the torment of fear.

Tonight when you go to sleep, let the Good Shepherd hold you. Say this "Sleeping Prayer": "I will lay down in peace and sleep, for Thou, oh Lord, will make sure that I dwell in **safety**. I am not alone. You are with me, and You never sleep or slumber. From now on, You are the one who goes before me and my family. I ask that You assign angels over me and my children: an angel on our left and an angel on our right. You will not leave me or forsake me. You are our fortress and strong tower. You are our safe place because You have wrapped Your eternal arms of strength around me. I will trust You." Read Deuteronomy 31:8, Psalm 4:8, Psalm 91, and Deuteronomy 33:27.

KEEP THE FAITH

One night, while Tommy was teetering between life and death, my husband and I were lying in bed, holding hands, and looking up at the ceiling. It was dark in the room and even darker in our lives. This wasn't the time to think only of myself. I was hurting, but so was my best friend. It was time to reach out to my husband as he had done for me so many times before. Somehow, by God's grace, I thought about his pain.

Let me tell you about my husband. My husband is a "man's man." He has the humility and wisdom of Denzel Washington, the die-hard spirit of Bruce Willis, and the humor of Steve Carrel. His son, his namesake, was about to die and leave him forever. I was broken to feel his pain. I asked, "Honey, what is one thing I can do to help you weather this crisis? Do you want a decent dinner *(please say no)*, more sex *(not really what I had in mind)*, a quiet household?" Notice I didn't say clean household! "Tell me one thing that I can do for you, lest I go mad with inactivity." It was my privilege to minister to him.

Listen to what he said. He thought pensively for a few seconds, then he grew ten feet tall, and my admiration for him grew even taller. He said confidently, "Keep the faith. If you keep the faith, then everything else will fall into place." Whoa! I told you he was wise!

I heeded his words. I prayed earnestly every day for the strength and wisdom to keep the faith. I could not trust my own reserve to pull me through this situation. I was flying to another universe and an ordinary tank of gas wasn't going to cut it. I needed eternal fuel instead of earthy fuel.

Pray for yourself right now: "God, give me Your strength and wisdom to keep the faith." Write this prayer on an index card. Put it in your car. Put it where you will see it every day and whisper the words. These are eleven words that will save your life—I am not exaggerating.

Day 38

SEX AND SUFFERING

B y God's grace and sheer willpower, we came together "as one flesh" pretty soon after Tommy's death. I don't remember if it was weeks or months. I would have preferred to ignore the entire subject, but there was someone else to consider: my best friend. I cheerfully, not grudgingly, invited him into my arms. I embraced him out of an act of my will to love him, not because I had any desire to connect.

Something wonderful and unexpected happened. Out of my sacrificial gift of love, God healed my heart. As I gave myself to my husband, somehow the sacrifice became a lifeline. At the same time, it rescued me, it freed me, and it fed me.

For a year, after the "explosion" wore off, I'd roll over into a fetal position and cry my eyes out. Five minutes before, I wasn't even thinking of Tommy, and then he was all I was thinking about. Somehow the hormonal joy blast mirrored the intense pain and sorrow. This cycle amazed and puzzled me. I always felt clean and refreshed after our time together and after my big cry. My heart was more whole afterwards than it was before we met between the sheets. Then I had a wild thought: what if the orgasm pushed the pain out of my body, like a contraction pushes the baby out of your womb?

If you don't have an earthly husband, you have the Lord as your husband. He will be better than ten husbands on earth. Trust that He cares for you and that He is as near as your whisper. At night, it can be lonely and scary. Hug a pillow and ask the Good Shepherd, to wrap His arms around you. It's not weird to think that! Did you know that the Shepherd slept across the gate to protect the sheep from wolves? He wants you to feel how much He loves you! If you have a husband, go to a quiet place, and ask God to fill you with His perfect love to love your husband. Ask God to make your love new and fresh. Ask Him to help you remember when your love was young and beautiful. Read Song of Solomon 4:1-16.

HELPING THE HURTING

One day, my Norwegian neighbor stopped by our house. Anne Marie was a woman I had tried to befriend over the years. I don't recall her phoning me to announce her visit. She just popped over like a friend. I opened the back door, glad to see a friendly face, and yet repulsed by the idea of making conversation. As I opened the door, her smile and concern said everything. She wanted to share my pain. She didn't know what to say, but she came anyway! And she came bearing gifts. She brought a bottle of perfume called "True Love." Then she left as quickly as she came. Her love left a strong fragrance in my house, and an even stronger impression on me.

What a brave woman! Even today, after all these years of losing Tommy and after all I know, I still hesitate to reach out. I'm basically a big chicken. I'd rather let someone suffer alone than risk the humiliation of being rejected. Anne Marie showed me that a friend can show she cares without a lot of fuss. She didn't have to stay all day or have grandiose words. She was light in my darkness for one shining moment. I knew she came to show me love. I honor her, and everyone who has stepped through the magic portal to comfort a not-so-close friend, with this page.

Let people love you. Let them hug you. Let their gifts remind you of your child. Let their love wash over you like a sweet spring rain.

You are going to be very tired. Write out a list of chores that people can help you with. Then when people offer to help, give them a choice of a couple of things and let them select the job they can do. Here are a few ideas: grab a few groceries, take clothes to the cleaners, clean your house, bring a meal, mow the lawn, weed the flowerbed, pick up your kids from school or the bus stop. If the helpers are teenagers, maybe they can make a CD of your child's favorite songs or send you photos from their phones.

Y'ALL ARE GONNA BE TIRED

Get ready for a big shocker. You are going to be tired for about five years! Forget volunteering for PTO. You now have an excuse to bow out! (See, here's one positive outcome already!) On the other hand, consider volunteering if it brings you tremendous joy **but** not at the expense of your family. In a normal life, we do 100 things a week; in depression, you can only do ten. Be wise and fruitful about what you do. Do only the **most** important things for the life and happiness of your family. Maybe getting a dog is more important for the kids than having a clean house. (Just wear sunglasses so you won't see the dust!)

An activity that used to take you fifteen minutes, will now take an hour or more. Don't beat yourself up. It is what it is. During the second year, you'll be able to do twelve things a week, then fifteen, then twenty, then thirty. For the next few years, get a maid! It's worth the investment. It pays back in compound interest! I didn't do this until year six. Big mistake.

Say no when people ask for your help, and don't feel guilty. Don't get mad; they just don't understand. You don't have to explain and remind everyone that you're tired because your child died. *Capisce*? (That's Italian for "Understand?")

Your kids are also going to be tired for about three to five years! Homework will be a challenge. You'll be lucky if they squeak by with Cs. Don't get mad at them for forgetting assignments or losing their cell phones for the third time. It's the grief that is making them forgetful. If they are having learning trouble at school, grief is the cause! Even if it is three years or five years after the death, take them to a learning specialist. Hold their hand; don't slap it. Show your support. Voice words of encouragement: "I know you are smart. You are having trouble now, but it won't always be this hard." (Pray the Confusion Prayer for them—from Chapter 48.)

Let go of perfection for yourself and your kids. (See Chapter 29.) Eternal things that you can't see are more important than the things you can see. Your relationship with your husband and children are more important then you getting your way on little things. If you are fighting with your family, ask yourself, "Will this matter in six months?" I know a mother and daughter who were disagreeing about a dress. The mother screamed, "You look like a @#$% slut in that @#$% dress. The daughter's face fell, and I knew in that moment the mother had lost her daughter over that stupid dress. If she had only told her "Little girl, I'm sorry that I said those things. Will you forgive me? If you want that dress, you can have it." Instead, the daughter moved out as soon as she could.

My daughter Mercy was taking gymnastics. She said, "Mommy, I am just too tired to do it anymore." She wasn't tired; she was in depression. I was afraid she would get behind and miss out on future opportunities. But God said, "Nancy, trust me. I will make it up to you." Do you know she made cheerleader without any gymnastic skills? In Texas, that is a full-on miracle!

Are you excited that you can "just say no," and pass on helping at VBS? The Good Shepherd has you on a different journey. You need not feel guilty. Let go of old baggage (not your husband). Have you ever seen anyone rolling suitcases up a mountain? It can't be done. Take this new compass. Embrace this new life instead of despising it. Old baggage will keep you from ascending the mountain the Good Shepherd has for you.

Hold the Good Shepherd with both hands and say no to extra activity. Say this prayer right now for your children: "May my children (list them by name) walk with You. May they be who You created them to be. May they lead others into Your Kingdom. Help them to grow in discernment. May they run from impurity and stand up for righteousness. May they grow in Your wisdom and in their authority in You, while retaining a submissive and humble spirit. May they find their identity in You."

Day **41**

HOW KIDS HANDLE
DEPRESSION

Do you want to know the root cause of teenage rebellion?
It's rejection. If you look back, several years through the
events of any teenager in rebellion, you will find several
major rejections or heart breaks. Death, divorce, and breakups
are the top three. Treat the rejection, and you avoid rebellion.
Help them heal their broken-heart and you avoid a phone call
from the police.

A broken heart is a hemorrhaging heart. How does a teen stop
a heart from bleeding? How do they make the pain go away?
Teenagers have a solution called alcohol and drugs. I call those
addictions false comforters. They work for a short while, but
they always come with a curse. If you treat the root and not
the rebellion, you will get great results. Take them to a grief
counselor rather than a parole officer. Hug them, even if they
don't want it. They are only rejecting you before you can reject
them. Surprise them!

Assume your children need help processing the death. We need help, why shouldn't they? We see them quiet, going on with life, and we assume they are ok. But I think it is a half-truth to think that kids can handle grief better than adults. Maybe they handle it better, but they still need help. If you can afford a good Christian counselor, who has a lot of experience dealing with children handling death, please take them for at least six months.

The greatest rejection for a child is to suffer through a divorce. Losing a parent is as tragic to a child as losing a child is to a parent. A divorce is a death to their world. God warns us, "For where envying and strife is, there is confusion and every evil work" (James 3:16 KJV, emphasis mine). It's normal if you're having trouble in your marriage, so treat it as soon as possible. If you go to a counselor immediately, you might only need to go two or three times! If you wait, the fault in the foundation gets bigger and bigger. May I be blunt? Sleep in separate rooms not separate houses! Why add more confusion and heartbreak by going through with a divorce; it only creates more problems. If you can stick by your spouse for 3-5 years, you **will** weather this terrible storm.

If you hold the hand of the Good Shepherd, He'll pull you through the eye of the needle. Nothing is impossible for Him.

Say this Marriage Prayer out loud: "Good Shepherd, my marriage needs You right now. If You come and hold both of us, I know we'll make it. Open our eyes to see each other's needs. Open our hearts to see each other's hurts. Help us to prefer each other. Do not let envy or strife get a foot in the door. Stop selfishness and self-pity in its tracks. Help us to prefer each other more than ourselves. Change us so we desire to listen more than to be heard."

SWEET RELIEF

When I got down and really depressed, I had a sure-fire quick fix. I dragged myself to my computer. I must have looked like the old woman in the Bible that was humped over for twelve years. I wrote a quick synopsis of my feelings; I shared my fears, hurts, and disappointments in one or two sentences. Then I simply asked for prayer from my closest friends, and sent it via my personal messenger named *e-mail*. Voila! As soon as I clicked "send mail," I got sweet relief. I love it! I did that for seven years, and it worked every time. Unbelievable! Awesome!

We are to bear one another's burdens. I think that sometimes my friends would cry so I didn't have to. It seemed that they bore some of the tears for me, and it is a miraculous cure.

You might not want to go on social networks for a while, since some people only posts happy events. When you are sad, definitely don't post on Facebook; it's better to share with a few of your closest friends. (Thanks Mirielle, Marcella, and Pam.)

Send an email to all of your friends, your child's friends, and your child's teachers asking them to write a story about your child and send it to you. Print and put them into a folder. Don't get discouraged or angry if you have to remind people, especially those who are still young. You can call people on the phone and listen to their story, take notes and later type them up. If your child is older, meet two or three of your child's friends at a restaurant. Tell them you don't want to cry—just laugh, and tell old stories. They miss your child too! You both can tell stories. If you meet several for lunch, they won't feel intimidated. Do this within the first three to six months.

Watch the movie *You've Got Mail* starring Meg Ryan and Tom Hanks. You'll love it! Maybe one day I will write another book about how movies helped heal me!

Day 43

GOD IS NOT A JEALOUS GOD

I know that the Bible says that God is jealous. But God isn't jealous in the traditional sense. God says He is jealous **for** us. What does that mean? God is zealous—eager—about protecting and providing the best for who is precious to Him. You are what is **precious** to God! It means His heart breaks when we hurt or when we hurt ourselves. It means that He loves you and me the same way we love our kids or our animals. We are jealous **for** them to make the right choices and jealous to provide the very best for them. We don't want our kids to settle for anything that is less. God is no less and no different.

If you believe that you understand your God and He does everything by the book, you better get another. He can't be God if He is so predictable. A friend said, "God is kinder, grander, holier, and lovelier than words can fully describe. He is God. He is mysterious, powerful, infinite, and uncreated. He has always been and always will be. His ways are always right, true, just, and full of a love that is purer than any understanding of purity we have. His beauty is as boundless as His infinity. He is matchless in love and passion for all of His creation."

Not only is He the maker of heaven and earth, but He is crazy-mad in love with you. He says to you, "I know what I'm doing. I have it all planned out—plans to take care of you, not abandon you; plans to give you the future you hope for. When you call on Me, I'll come running. When you pray to Me, I'll listen. When you come looking for Me, you'll find Me. Yes, when you get serious about finding Me and want it more than anything else, I'll make sure you won't be disappointed." (See Jeremiah 29:11-13.) God's decree is, "I'll turn things around for you."

Isn't that a wonderful promise and words of affection? Ask Him to help you. Believe it. Write it on an index card, put it where you will see it, and whisper it up as a prayer of trust and understanding: "Lord, now I understand that You aren't jealous like a man; You are jealous **for** my happiness! Establish Your presence in me and let Your Presence bring peace to my spirit, soul, and body. Lord, help me to trust You even when I don't see or understand the plan. Thank You that I don't have to do live alone. You are with me and walking in my every footprint. Live and breathe through me. Be in my heart, my feet, my hands. Help me to see that You delight in me just the way I am."

ONLY JOB LOST IT ALL

It seemed to me that two years had passed when one day I was singing a song that said, "I gave it all up for you." In my heart I said, "Lord, I gave it all up for You when I gave You Tommy." Then I heard my sweet Daddy God in heaven politely say one word: "All?" I realized I only **felt** like I lost everything; in reality, I had only lost one precious thing in my privileged life. Only Job can say he lost everything! He lost all his children, all his property, all his investments, all his employees, and his health. The Lord showed me a root of self-pity and deceit that was wedged between the concrete joints in my heart. I asked Him to pull up the root and keep revealing more. I quickly agreed with the thought and realized I had a lot to be grateful for in my life.

It was as if a valve had been opened and pus was allowed to drain out of my heart. I could breathe deeper than I had before. I didn't feel quite so isolated from the world. I thought I was the **only one** who had a loss. The truth is everyone has a great pain and loss that they have to live with. I didn't feel like the whole world had been taken away from me. I felt free for the first time in two years. "...and you will know the truth, and the truth will make you free" (John 8:32 NASB).

This prescription brings a balance to focusing on our pain. I didn't get the realization until two years had passed. This realization may be too soon for you, but I think in the journey of healing there comes a fork in the road where we must make a choice. One road beckons us to let go, to move forward to the great things that lie ahead; the other road yells at us to hold onto the "right" of being in pain. It forces us to take ownership of our pain. We become a slave to the pain while striving to keep our child's memory alive and dropping hints about our child to others. The pain now controls us.

If you find yourself experiencing a lot of health issues, it may be a signal that you got off on the wrong road. Health issues and body pains can be the body's way of telling us that there are some attitudes in the heart that we need to address.

Sit and journal without a mask; write how you really feel. Let the pain, anger, bitterness, self-pity, and resentment rise to the surface like dross from silver's refining fire. Just like we need to let vomit come to the surface, so we must get the ugliness out of our hearts. Remember He is a good, loving, and perfect Daddy God who wants the best for you.

YOU ARE LIKE MARY THE MOTHER OF JESUS

The Bible records the words of the angel to Mary: "'Greetings, you who are highly favored! The Lord is with you.' Mary was greatly troubled at his words and wondered what kind of greeting this might be... 'Do not be afraid, Mary; you have found favor with God. You will conceive and give birth to a son, and you are to call him Jesus...This child is destined to cause the falling and rising of many in Israel...so that the thoughts of many hearts will be revealed. And a sword will pierce your own soul too'" (Luke 1:28-31; 2:34-35 NIV).

I know you don't feel highly favored. You feel abandoned, rejected, and crushed. You must believe by faith that you are highly favored if the Good Shepherd allowed you to walk the road of suffering alongside Him. Out of all the mothers in the world, He chose **you** to be your child's mommy. Maybe, just like Mary, you were chosen for this assignment. You didn't sign up for it; He picked you because He could trust you.

Could it be that God knew it would thrust a sword into your heart? It broke His heart, but many more lives were at stake. Your child's life was destined to cause the rising and falling of many, so that the thoughts of many hearts would be revealed. Maybe our nation was at a crossroad and they needed a shaking: a reason to choose God over the other gods of this world. As the mom, you would be denied a momentary future with your son so that heaven would be secured for others. Your heart is momentarily broken, so that others can be made whole.

Here's some good news. Dear One, your Heavenly Father will give you the desires of your heart on this side of heaven. He will give you a hope and a future on earth today. If you ask Him, He will not leave you broken; He will make you brand new. I don't know how, but this I am sure; He will make up our losses to us somehow someway. It will be above and beyond anything we could ever imagine.

I want you to do an exercise. Take a deep breath and inhale this truth into your lungs three times. Say, "My Father God will give me a good life here." Say it at least three times every day, and breathe so deeply that your toes feel it. Write it on an index card, and put it where you will see it often.

IF YOU TOUCH

I remember having a chat with God. I was a new mother with my first child. I was overwhelmed with love for her and distraught with the thought that she could die. I remember sitting on the side of our whirlpool tub. I clearly recall saying to my Father, "If one of my kids dies, I am going to hate You. Let's get that on the table. I might as well repent up front because I know I will hate You."

Basically, I said in my native Texas drawl, "I love my kids so much that if You touch 'em, I'll kill Ya. I'll kill Ya with my own bare hands." Ha! Ha! This was not anything shocking to my Father God; He already knew how I felt. I think He made me raw and honest for His daily laughter. I needed to say it to myself. I needed to see that my heart was a dormant volcano just waiting for the right conditions.

After Tommy died, some weeks after his funeral, I was literally dragging myself to stay alive. I only functioned for my three other kids. As my Father would have it, I found myself sitting on the same bathtub. I said, "Loooord, if there were any other God, I sure would be giving him a chance. This is so hard!"

Then I said the magic words. "Nevertheless, there is nowhere else to go; You have the words of eternal life. Therefore, I choose You." (See John 6:68.) I blessed Him so much that day! I chose to give Him **true love** not because I got what I wanted but because of who **He is!** I also blessed myself. I tapped into the Giver of Life and healing. I gave myself spiritual CPR, and it was at that moment that I began to breathe and come back to life. I slept so deep that night that when I awoke, my mind was more clear and alert.

Hang on to your Heavenly Father. Believe He is working the worst situations into something good. He is a good Father and He has you in the palm of His hand. If you ask Him, He will heal you **and** your family. One day, He will show His grand plan for your family.

RAW AND OPEN

I want to expound on two ideas of being raw and honest with God. I hope it brings truth and light. Many people are afraid to be totally honest with God. They are afraid that He'll hurl down bolts of lightning. But our God in heaven doesn't have an ego; He doesn't pout and get even. He doesn't give us the silent treatment. Why? Because He is a good Daddy, and He loves us. God sees our hearts, so why put up any pretense?

There is a balance. Just because we **can** get mad at God doesn't give us a right to throw poop or daggers at Him. For example, my teenager told me once, "I hate you! I hate you so much! I could stab you." I knew she didn't really mean it. I had only told her that she couldn't go to the mall. Today, she and I have a howling laugh at her comment.

When our kids throw temper tantrums, we don't stop loving them. If we can overlook their immaturity, how much more will our heavenly Father do the same thing? He's perfect and we're not. If we have an ounce of patience, He has an ocean full. If we love our kids no matter what they do or say to us, our heavenly Father feels the same towards us.

After ten years of ranting and raving, I am ready to grow up. I have learned to share my hurt and confusion with God without chewing Him out.

I think God is totally enthralled with someone who responds to Him with honesty and yet with discretion. The movie *Ever After*, starring Drew Barrymore, totally reflects my idea. Drew is Cinderella and her honesty makes her the apple of the prince's affection. I love the scene where he says to her, "How do you do it?" She says, "Do what?" He responds, "Live with such passion every day!"

Do you know that your Father in Heaven is ravished with **you?** You don't have to be perfect. You don't have to be anything other than yourself. He is inviting you to be in His kingly family which would make you the daughter of the King! Say yes! Say yes!

I TOLD GOD I WAS ANGRY
BY JESSICA SHAVER

I told God I was angry.
I thought He'd be surprised.
I thought I'd keep hostility
quite cleverly disguised.

I told the Lord I hate Him
I told Him that I hurt.
I told Him that He isn't fair,
He's treated me like dirt.

I told God I was angry
but I'm the one surprised.
"What I've known all along," He said,
"you've finally realized.

"At last you have admitted
what's really in your heart.
Dishonesty, not anger,
was keeping us apart.

"Even when you hate Me
I don't stop loving you.
Before you can receive that love,
you must confess what's true.

"In telling me the anger
you genuinely feel,
It loses power over you,
permitting you to heal."

I told God I was sorry,
and He's forgiven me.
The truth that I was angry
has finally set me free.

PUSH! PUSH! PUSH!

ush! Push! **Push!** During childbirth, the coach told me to push through the pain. "Don't stop pushing because something needs to come out."

The grieving process was similar to childbirth. I needed to push through the pain. Push through the anger. Push through the hurt. Push through the depression. Don't stop. Don't ignore the pain. Keep pushing it out. Unlike childbirth, you won't ever get over it, but you can get through it.

How did I push through the pain? I began my crying session by inviting the Lord to cry with me. If I cried by myself, it resulted in an empty temper tantrum. If I invited the Lord to hold my hand, I felt refreshed.

"I hurt, God...take it away." Puuush your hurt toward heaven! As you call out to Him, you're pushing the hurt out of your body.

"I'm mad at you, God...take it away." Puuush your anger onto God. Don't hold on to it. Push it out!

"I miss my child so much." Puuush your sadness out.

Cast your burdens upon Him for He cares for you. (See 1 Peter 5:7.) As you continue to push out the pain, God is pulling the pain out of your heart. When you feel the urge, **push! Push! Push!**

Take His hand and pray this Prayer for Grief and Sorrow: "Lord, nothing makes sense anymore. Everything that I thought was truth got rocked. Help me to hold on to You for dear life! Lord, remove all **confusion** from my spirit, soul and body. I release it to You now. (Breathe in and out.) Lift the fog off my mind. Give me Your clarity and understanding. Bring my body, my heart, my lungs, my immune system, my chemistry, my _____ into Your perfect, divine order. Break the stronghold that grief and sorrow have over my life and my family. Push today's anxiety away from me. **Impart Your resurrection life** into my innermost being. Deposit hope into the core of my being. Plant the seed of Your amazing love into every cell of my spirit, soul, and body, and make it grow in exponential ways. Blow Your Life into the places that are dark and sad and lifeless. I receive Your shield of grace and the light of Your protection." (Of course, you can insert any family member in this prayer.)

HEALED STITCH BY STITCH

Each time I felt the sensation of pain, I pushed it out onto the Good Shepherd, and each time I pushed out the pain, He mended my heart. Every time I pushed out the sorrow, He repaired my broken heart stitch by stitch.

The more I pressed into Him by allowing myself to cry with prayer, the more stitches He was able to make. And the more stitches He was allowed to make, the more quickly I felt like I was back to normal. I truly believe that my overall healing was quicker and more thorough because I pressed into God with crying prayers.

These signals of pain were gifts from God. He used the sensation of pain as a flag that marked the spot He wanted to remove. He could only remove the spot of pain if I pushed it out with prayer.

As you feel hurt, visualize His finger marking a spot for you to process. Verbalize your pain into a short, prayerful sentence. Lift up your hurt to Him so He can stitch your heart. The Good

Shepherd is using each tear to stitch your heart little by little. His finger marks the spot of mercy.

I know it sounds like an impossible dream to feel normal again. I promise if you hold sorrow in one hand and your Father in the other, you will feel normal again. He intends to mend you, stitch by stitch. Say this Prayer of Admittance out loud: "God of the Universe, help me not to deny my pain but to bring it to You. Give me the courage to take off any masks that I am clinging to. I need You just to make it through one day. Transfer Your strength and refreshing into me. I surrender to You. I depend on You. Let Your presence flow in around me and my family today. Be the strength of my family. Be my family's rock to lean on. Be real to them."

YOU ARE NOT RUNNING ALONE

Grieving is a process. I had good moments and bad moments. One minute I was fine; the next minute I was sad. I had a roller coaster of emotions several times during the day. My life was scary.

I calmed myself by imagining my healing as a relay race where the Father and I passed a baton. I imagined, "Runners, to your mark. Go!" The sound of the gun set me free to run as hard as I could. Then came my turn to pass the baton. Sometimes, I gladly passed the baton to the Father. He gently grabbed it and ran with all His might!

If I got scared and held onto the baton, we lost the race, but if I chose to give the baton away, we won! My Father did not leave me to run alone; in fact, He ran beside me, cheering and panting along the way.

I saw grieving as passing the baton. As I made myself sit with Him and cry, I could feel the pain being lifted out of my heart. If

I refused to deal with the pain, I held the pain inside my heart. I was miserable until I chose to pass my pain to Him. Soon I came to realize that if I gladly chose to cry and get alone with Him, the pain would pass.

You are in the race of your life, but you are not alone. Picture Him cheering you onward. Run for the prize and pray this Prayer of Strength: "Lord of all the heavens, I am running on empty. Be my strength today. Let Your power pulsate through me. I need Your presence because You are the source of life and goodness. Refresh my spirit, soul, and body. Wash over me. Heal my heart and mind. Only You, can help me keep calm and carry on."

HOW TO LET GO OF THE PAIN

I learned to let go of the pain by holding the Father in one hand and holding sorrow in the other. When I allowed myself time to grieve, I allowed myself time to heal. I released my tears like I would release a balloon toward heaven. Crying released the pain out of my heart. As I cried, the pain gradually floated away.

Conversely, I felt that if I ignored the pain, I'd push the pain deeper into my heart. I imagined pushing a large balloon into my heart. Then the balloon was trapped inside my heart waiting for the next trauma so it could burst. I saw unresolved pain as a ticking time bomb.

I believed that if I refused to deal with the pain that day, I would just have hell to pay later and with compound interest! I began to recognize the impulse to cry, and I found time to grieve. I even watched a movie or played a CD that helped me relax and cry. I know this seems weird, but I almost had to help myself "get in the mood" to cry.

Eventually, I began to welcome the grieving signals because I knew it meant one hole of my Swiss cheese heart would be filled. I got some Kleenex and some chocolate and poured my pain into the Father's lap. The chocolate was my reward.

Time doesn't heal; time with God does. I know you are hurting beyond any words that I could transcribe. But God understands your sorrow. At one point in His life, He had exceeding sorrow even to the point of sweating blood. There is nothing that you can say that will shock Him. He cares for you. He loves you. Be a little girl again. Climb into your heavenly Daddy's lap, and release your tears.

"Father God, I am missing _____ so much that my heart literally hurts. Thank You for being near to the broken-hearted. Bind up my broken heart. (In your mind's eye, see Him binding your broken heart.) Thank You that You won't turn me away. You are the Healer. Wrap Your Spirit around me with the comfort of Your love. There is such a void without my child. Would You come and fill the void that I feel? Fill me. Fill me. Fill me to overflowing." Wait for Him to fill you. Breathe in and drink in His sweetness. You might want to say this prayer every day for a while.

EVERY DAY IS GREAT FAITH

In our Heavenly Father's economy, every day that you get out of bed, you are demonstrating that today will be a better day. He considers your simple routines as a demonstration of your faith. Likewise, every day that you brush your teeth, you are smiling with your faith. Everyday that you put one leg into your pants, you are walking out your great faith.

Our Father knows that the simplest acts of routine are not so simple to the hurting. This is a crude analogy but He realizes that we feel like crap and yet we keep trudging onward. He is honored with our actions. He even rewards us for every cup of cold water that we give to one another. He considers the simplest acts of survival as acts of love and worship to Him.

He could think, "So, you lost a child, deal with it!" But He's **not** a mean taskmaster. He's a loving Father who wants to applaud us as we stumble along with our first steps in this new walk of faith. He knows it is hard, but He has confidence in you! He knows that you can make it with Him by your side. He is your number one fan!

You may resent that simple acts are so difficult to execute, but realize that they don't go unnoticed. He remembers them all and records them in a book. Try to imagine your reward for every meal that you prepare.

Wow! Say this to yourself: "The God of the Universe has confidence in me!" Maybe no one had confidence in you growing up, but God does! Ask Him to plant this truth deep down in your inner being and to water it and cause it to produce great fruit!

"Therefore, since we have so great a cloud of witnesses surrounding us, let us also lay aside every encumbrance and the sin which so easily entangles us, and let us run with endurance the race that is set before us, fixing our eyes on Jesus, the author and perfecter of faith, who for the joy set before Him endured the cross, despising the shame, and has sat down at the right hand of the throne of God" (Hebrews 12:1-3 NASB).

WHEN YOUR HEART HAS BEEN SHATTERED

If you can love even after your heart has been shattered, then that is true love. Consider this passage. You may remember hearing it as a child. Here is my modern rendition: If you love those who love you, what reward will you get? (Nothing.) Are not even thieves doing that? And if you greet only your friend, what are you doing more than others? Do not even gangsters do that? (See Matthew 5:46-47.)

Let's apply this concept to our Heavenly Father. If we only love Him because He's given us everything we ever asked for, what kind of love is that? (Nothing.) Even infidels worship those that are good to them. But if we can get past ourselves and just love Him for **who** He is, rather than for **what** He gives, then we are exhibiting real love.

God is not an ego-maniac. He knows a secret that I am going to expose! "A man reaps what he sows...whoever sows to please the Spirit, from the Spirit will reap eternal life. Let us not become weary in doing good, for at the proper time we will reap a harvest if we do not give up" (Galatians 6:6-9 NIV). If you sow love, you reap love. If you sow love to the Father, you reap exponential love. If we love God and others, then we are healing ourselves. When we give out love, we are bringing it back onto ourselves! Giving love to God and others heals our hearts to the core.

I wear a perfume called "True Love" as a reminder of this. This is the perfume from Anne Marie in Chapter 39. Go out and buy a fragrance that is named something extraordinary and is symbolic for you. Look for little tokens—signs from God—that He hears you and He cares for you. His love is deeper than any love found on earth. It is higher than heavens, and He has all this loved saved up for you!

Pray this Prayer for Vision: "Give me eyes to see, ears to hear, and a heart to perceive that You are with me and that I am not walking alone. Shine Your light so that I don't grope in the darkness. Open my ears to hear Your still, small, sweet voice. Open my mouth to speak the truth in love. Open my eyes to see Your path that You have set out for me. Help me to perceive Your ways. Awaken me to feel alive again."

ERASER

If I were forced to name one prescription for healing after experiencing a terrible trauma, it would be this thought: We suffered a terrible loss because God chose us as secret agents for a special mission that would change the world.

I know it's corny, and I don't have any proof; I just believed it by faith in the core of my being. This idea gave me something to hope for.

I saw a movie that demonstrated my perspective. In the movie Eraser, starring Arnold Schwarzenegger and Vanessa Williams, the female character enters the federal witness protection program. Arnold (God) must erase her old life so she can participate with him to stop evil from triumphing. He takes her away from a normal, mundane, safe life to carry her through a scary and uncertain present, so that the world would be a better place in the future. She resists the new scary life, but he shows her that without her testimony, certain evil will continue to corrupt the world and the people she loves. Reluctantly, she accepts.

There is a very powerful moment in the movie; it still makes me cry. In order to protect her, Arnold must erase her past. She makes the comment, "'Wow, you are burning everything that I am." He corrects her. "These things are not who you are; you are who you are on the inside." Later she discovers that what she thought would kill her actually made her a more courageous and more compassionate human being. In essence, he rescued her from herself.

After Tommy died, something weird happened; our life turned upside down. It was as if we were put in the witness protection plan and assumed a new identity. We were offered a new job, moved across town, started new schools, built a new house, bought new furniture, and met new friends. The only thing we kept from our old life was our car. A year later, I took care of that too: I wrecked it!

Likewise, you have been chosen for a special assignment. Trust me; our Heavenly Father will take your pain and turn it around for a great purpose. No matter what happened to you, our magnificent Father God will use your painful event and make it a powerful part of His grand plan. You've got to believe that. Swallow that idea into the soul of your being. If you're like most people, you didn't accept your assignment. You probably said to yourself, "Why me? I didn't sign up for this!" Like Vanessa from the movie Eraser, we resist losing our comfortable life, for the scary life of uncertainty.

Like in the movie The Matrix, you have the choice to take the red pill or the blue pill. Look into the heart of the One who called you. Don't think about your pain; think about the world's gain.

The One who holds out the red pill is the One who holds the words of eternal life. Your testimony is crucial. The only way the mission will be successful is if you reluctantly accept. Remember what Jesus said, "...not My will but Thine be done" (Luke 22:42 KJV). If you can say "Thy will be done" however reluctantly, then the mission is accomplished.

This mission is not impossible. You won't be alone. If you choose to accept this mission, it will be incredible. What you think will kill you will actually give you an abundant life. Our Father takes our invisible pain and uses it to the world's gain. He transforms our sacrifices into instruments of healing. Tell Him that you'll take the mission. Ask Him to use you and your family for great exploits.

POLLYANNA

For me, the hardest aspect of grieving was that I didn't like to be unhappy. As a child, my family nickname was "Sunshine." Sometimes people teased me by calling me Pollyanna. On the other hand, if something sad happened in a movie, I cried easily. Hallmark commercials use to make me bawl like a baby. My friends took me to see the movie Ice Castles in the 80s just to see me cry!

Then in 1999, Pollyanna became Sybil. My life turned upside down. The negative emotions scared me to death: no pun intended. The pain was so intense that sometimes it was hard to breathe. Pain followed me like a shadow. I wanted to get in a car and run, but I knew the pain would follow me there.

I wanted to deny the pain by being busy. Praise God for a little lady named Oprah Winfrey. Remember how she shared about her abuse? She taught us that we must deal with pain, or it gets trapped inside of us. If we didn't deal with the pain, it would bite us in the butt. It can manifest as anger, bitterness, and grumpiness. The pain can become physical ailments. When we ignore the pain, we are living in denial and deceiving ourselves. We are big, fat liars.

I couldn't trust my ability to get me through this situation because I didn't know how the heck to grieve properly. So, I phoned a friend, Jay, and I talked to him frequently to get direction and encouragement. During the course of the day, I dialogued with God just like He was my friend. I had an honest relationship with Him. (See Chapter 10: Dialoguing With God.)

When I first started the journey of grieving, it looked very messy. I was a mess, but my Heavenly Father didn't care how I looked. He loved me and held me close. He will do the same for you if you ask Him. I have come a long way in my healing, but healing is like good lasagna: there are always layers, and the process takes time.

Take a nap with God. Hold His hand. Ask Him to help you put down the masks. The pain can feel like we are hemorrhaging, so we seek false comforters. God is the only true healer. He is near to the broken-hearted. Pray this prayer for your emotions: "Father God, I feel like I am falling. Hold me! Hug Me! Here I am again with so much pain that I could burst. I release it to You. (Imagine it evaporating out of you.) Lord, where I have shut down my emotions, gradually help me to feel again. Where my emotions are out of control, stop them with the force of Your peace. Cause my emotions to be transformed into productivity. Help me to trust You and know that I don't have to be perfect even in my grieving. Heal me through and through. Renew my heart, body, and mind into perfect wholeness and happiness."

ANTI-DEPRESSANTS

I was too proud and clueless when it came to taking antidepressants. Remember the song by Helen Reddy "I Am Woman Hear Me Roar!"? Boy, could I roar! What I didn't know was that the anger, fits of rage, and forgetfulness were warning flags telling me that I needed medicine. These issues were a megaphone calling for help, but I was stressed. A better name for the pills would be "anti-stressants."

I also felt guilty for needing a crutch. I was raised to believe that "I can do all things through Christ who strengthens me" (Philippians 4:13 NKJV). My sweet mom and dear mother-in-law had some great words of wisdom for me. They told me that the pills were a gift from God. My friend Kendra compared antidepressants to insulin for a diabetic. Reluctantly, I took them. What a wonderful difference the pills made!

I had another weird health issue. I would awake at 3:00 a.m., bright-eyed and bushy-tailed. When your body sleeps, it heals the deep tissues of the body. The pills helped me sleep through the night. I ultimately took the pills for my family. I know people who have benefited from the medicine, and subsequently decided to get off the pills. Then they spiral down into abnormal behavior. Family members beg them to take their medicine. I didn't want to become a nuisance to my family, and I didn't want to hurt them. In the end, I decided that if taking a silly pill was such an easy thing, I could do it for my family's happiness. Why not do it?

Here's the balance. The pills were only a bandage for the wound. Real healing came from crying and allowing God to dig out the fear, bitterness, rejection, etc. from my soul. I think medicine and meditation complemented each other as long as I meditated on God, not on my problems.

What health issues do you have? It's ok. These weird things that are happening to your body are a result of a big trauma in your life. Take His hand and say out loud, "Lord, cause all shock and trauma to be released out of my spirit, soul, and body. Take every trace of confusion out of me, and renew my spirit, soul, and body to wholeness and happiness as You originally designed. Where my body glands, chemistry, or immune system is out of whack, command it to align into Your perfect order and balance. Release Your glory and light into my life. Lead me in Your love forevermore. Thank You that You promise to work things together for good."

Day **58**

THE HEART WILL SPEAK

Mankind judges us by our outward appearance, but our Heavenly Father looks at the condition of hearts. (See 1 Samuel 16:7.) The only hope we have of changing is to confess our need to our Daddy in heaven and let Him deal with it. God doesn't help those who help themselves; He helps those that ask Him! He's a gentleman, and He won't tread where He's not invited.

Picture this idea. Our hearts are the soil of our soul, and our words are the flowers that grow out of our soil. Our Father is a gardener. He knows that no soil is perfect. There's always room for some fertilizer. If a plant has contaminated soil, the flower will be ugly, and the fruit will be bitter. When we gossip, lie, brag, sass, snap, or judge, it is an indicator that the soul is contaminated. The only fix is to allow the Heavenly Gardener to add more of Himself to bring wholeness to the soil.

Listen to the words in your heart and mind. Are your thoughts bitter, sassy, and mean? Don't get discouraged. Be encouraged that your Heavenly Father is a wonderful gardener and He has the magic formula for miracle growth. The formula is casting all your problems upon Him for He cares for you. Invite Him to look at your garden. Don't be embarrassed by the amount of weeds you have. Remember, there are one billion of us with the same problem. Ask Him to pull out each weed as He finds it.

If there is something negative that keeps rolling around in your mind, write it down and ask God to stop this train of thought. Then burn it! Burn it as a symbol that God will burn up all the weeds that seek to choke out the happiness in your life.

I think it really helps to pray this "Prayer of Releasing" out loud: "Lord of heaven, I need Your presence because You are the source of life and goodness. Refresh my spirit, soul, and body. Wash over me. Heal my heart and mind. By your authority, stop the compulsive thoughts that keep coming into my mind, or show me the root cause. I release my worries of_____. I release fears of _____. I release my bitterness tied to_____. You said to give You all my trouble. So I take this log off my shoulder, and I give it to You. Deliver me from all negative tendencies that I inherited from my family such as bitterness, worrying, or being fearful. I choose to lift up my eyes towards heaven, because my help comes from You, the maker of heaven and earth." Read Psalm 121.

GOD CARES FOR YOU

I know you have one child in heaven, but you can't worry about your future or it will rob you of your future! If you give your Father God in heaven your life, then there's no need to fear the future. God's got the whole world at His fingertips. Look at the birds, free and unfettered, not tied down to a job description, careless in the care of God. And yet, your Heavenly Father cares for each one. He knows when one of His little sparrows falls to the ground. And you count for **far more** to Him than the birds. (See Matthew 6:26-28 MSG.)

You and your family are more precious to Him than all the stars in the heavens. Take a deep breath and breathe a sigh of relief— no more worries about the future. Your Father is on the throne ready to move heaven and earth just for you. "...anyone who wants to approach God must believe that he exists and that he cares enough to respond to those who seek him" (Hebrews 11:6 MSG).

After my son died, I had no clue how to grieve. No one teaches you how to do it. I wanted to do it well, so it wouldn't plague me the rest of my life. I began studying how other people handled death with hope. I discovered Corrie ten Boom. She lived in Holland during World War ll. She hid Jewish families in her house but was eventually sent to Ravensbruck—the worst concentration camp for women in Germany. Miracles happened in the camp, but almost everyone in her family died including her beloved sister, Betsy. She has written over twenty-five books, and I have read every one of them! I practically have a PhD in studying Corrie ten Boom! She doesn't gloss over suffering, and she doesn't feel sorry for herself either.

Corrie has traveled to over sixty countries as an eighty-year-old woman to share the lessons she has learned. She is now walking the streets of gold, hand-in-hand, with her sister Betsy. Corrie is one of my modern-day heroes. A movie called The *Hiding Place* has been made of her life.

Another hero of mine is lmmaculée llibagiza. She wrote a book called Left to Tell: *Discovering God Amidst the Rwandan Holocaust*. It's a fabulous book but scary and intense at times. It may be too soon for you to read. Try it in two to three years. You won't be able to put it down. The author's courage will truly inspire you. She is still alive, and I hope to meet her one day.

The stories of these lives moved me out of pity into a place of truth. It was true that I had a son that went to heaven, but I hadn't suffered like those women. They taught me how to handle my grief and suffering. God knows when the little birds fall to the ground. How much more will He know when we have our children in heaven? His eye is on the sparrow, and His eye is watching you and our children in heaven. I know you are wondering why God didn't move heaven and earth to save your child. Maybe He saved them ten times before from other tragedies. We will never know until we get to that Golden City.

Check out some You Tube videos of Corrie ten Boom. She is adorable. Here are a few books by Corrie ten Boom that I think you will like: *He Cares for You, Amazing Love, In My Father's House,* and *Life Lessons from the Hiding Place.*

GOD ISN'T PICKING ON YOU—MAYBE HE'S PICKING YOU OUT

I know you've been asking yourself, "What did I **ever** do to deserve this?" "Why is God punishing me?" "Why did You abandon me, God?" God is not rejecting you or punishing you. Maybe He knew you could handle it. God doesn't cause tragedy, but sometimes He does have to painfully allow it, and it breaks His heart to do it! But He promises to turn the tragedy around so that a million wonderful things come out of it. We know that all that happens to us is working for our good if we love God and are fitting into His plans. (See Romans 8:28.)

God is a merciful, loving God who gave His only son because it was the **only** option He had to save the rest of us. Jesus did it because **He** wanted to please His Father, and He didn't want to be an orphan. He wanted brothers and sisters! Sometimes a few have to suffer for the good of mankind. Is that so bad? God doesn't just have me to think about it; He has to look out for the wellbeing of the entire world and multiple generations. God sees 10,000 years from now. He has a greater good in mind for your suffering. Maybe Tommy's life and death will influence someone to go into the medical field and discover a cure for cancer!

The Bible compares God to a silversmith who will sit as a refiner and purifier of silver. Did you know that a silversmith purifies silver of impurities in a high heat and he knows just the right temperature for each piece of silver? He must **sit** with his silver and constantly keep watch over it while he is making it. He wouldn't dream of rejecting or walking away from his creation or else the silver would burn and be ruined forever. The silversmith **sits** near the silver because his work is complete when he can see his reflection in the silver.

Maybe God chose your family because He knew He would see Himself in your situation. He could count on your family changing your community. Corrie ten Boom, survivor of a Nazi concentration camp in 1944, said,

> Yet what we suffer now is nothing compared to the glory He will reveal to us later. If we are His children then we are heirs to His kingdom and if we share in His glory, we will share in His sufferings. These troubles and sufferings of ours will result in God's richest blessing upon us forever and ever! So we do not look at what we can see right now, the troubles all around us, but we look forward to the joys in heaven which we have not yet seen. The troubles will soon be over, but the joys to come will last forever. [2]

---

[2] Pam Rosewell Moore, *Life Lessons from Corrie ten Boom,* (Bloomington, MN: Chosen Books, 1973), 145.

Have you ordered a book written by Corrie ten Boom? Oh, how I wish you would!

Write this out and put it on your refrigerator: "The Heavenly Father will send us His Spirit, the Comforter, to help us with our daily problems and in our praying. For we don't even know what we should pray for nor how to pray as we should, but the Holy Spirit prays for us with such feeling that it cannot be expressed in words. And the Father who knows all hearts knows, of course, what the Spirit is saying as He pleads for us in harmony with God's own will. And we know that all that happens to us is working for our good if we love God and are fitting into His plans." (See Romans 8:26-28.)

WHAT IS HEAVEN LIKE?

In our journey of healing, Lee, a friend and co-worker of my husband's, gave us an amazing little book. We credit this book as one of the most influential contributors toward our healing. Little did Lee know that Tom bought a case of these books and gave them to anyone he knew who had a loved one die. *My Dream of Heaven*, by Rebecca Springer, was written around 1900. In the book, Ms. Springer writes about her experiences in heaven while she was in a coma. The Billy Graham society has endorsed the book.

It gives a glimpse of a day in the life of heaven. My favorite part was learning what children and babies do in heaven. She wrote about ordinary people who were not necessarily known on earth, but in heaven they were celebrities! She talked about seeing an older woman who looked so radiant and yet so familiar; it was her mother as a young woman! She talked about fields of flowers, magnificent mansions, and majestic mountains. I only read one paragraph before bed so I could prolong the joy and surprises as much as possible. I called it the chocolate mint on my pillow.

I am glad to know that heaven will be an exciting place to live. We won't be playing harps on clouds; we will be flying to other galaxies! Learning doesn't stop in heaven; we are still studying the universe, the human body, and every subject that can be thought of. If people weren't able to attend a university, they will be able to study any subject of their heart's desire. In fact, we can have as many degrees as we want! There are no limits in heaven when it comes to learning or exploring.

When it is our time to enter the gates of heaven, we will be side-by-side with our children and loved ones in heaven forevermore. Nothing will ever separate us from them again. Your child is getting to know **all** of your relatives, on both sides of the family, from every generation. One day, he will introduce them to you. Heaven is real, and our children are experiencing it right now! I daily ask God to introduce Tommy to famous people from the Bible and in history. Today let it be Joan of Arc.

When I want Tommy to know that I am thinking about him, I ask God to read my heart, write it out, and give it to him. God is so creative, He might write it in flowers! As I said before, when I want Tommy to be a part of a special event on earth, I ask God to record it or open the curtains of heaven so that he can watch it with a great many other witnesses and relatives down the ages.

I wonder what our kids are doing right now. Maybe your son is walking on the sun! Or your daughter is playing with a lion family. My nephew Cameron and Tommy are building me a magnificent theater complex because as you can tell, I love movies. I suggest that you get your own copy of *My Dream of Heaven*.

WHY DO CHILDREN DIE?

A fter reading the book *My Dream of Heaven*, by Elizabeth Springer, I had a great revelation. I can pass the secret on to you so that you can tell others. This secret is the kind of jewel that you want to ponder in your heart and share with others when the time is right.

Take a moment to think about eternity. Close your eyes and picture, or imagine, eternity. That is considerably longer than 10,000 years. Longer than ten million years. Longer than 100 million years. Eternity is a very, very, very long time; it is forever. Now imagine eternity as 100 million times 100 million years **without** babies, children, teenagers or young people! Yuck! That would be awful. That would be like having Christmas without any kids. That would be so boring. Who wants to spend eternity with a bunch of old people? Ha! Ha!

God told us that we need to have the heart of a child: the kind of heart that is loving, joyful, and kind. I surmise that God wants to spend heaven with a bunch of cute little guys and gals. God enjoys running, jumping, and skipping with them! I think He likes their noise, their messes, and their enthusiasm.

I know it's hard to think that we have to be without our kids while heaven gets to enjoy them, but we **will see them again**. Children go to heaven. They know in their hearts that they need a Savior. They are born knowing they are weak and God is strong. They talk to God when they are swinging, surfing, boating, painting, or playing sports. Don't worry about if they've got it all worked out with God. Jesus said He is the door to heaven, so when they came knocking, He opened it gladly.

Take another minute to imagine heaven without any children or young people. Wouldn't that be boring? Remember that there is no pain or suffering in heaven. When you can, tell God it's ok that He has your child. Tell your Father God that you "forgive" Him. Tell Him that you know your child is safe and having fun. Think of something wild and crazy that your child could be doing in heaven right now! What is he doing? I think my Tommy is flying to new planets without a space suit and playing guitar in a rock band! Just think: you can breathe underwater in heaven without coming up for air!

I promise the book *My Dream of Heaven* will expand your thinking about heaven. Read it to your kids at bedtime! They will **love** it!

WHAT IF YOUR CHILD COMMITTED SUICIDE OR OVERDOSED ON DRUGS?

What if your child died in an alcohol or drug-related death? What if they committed suicide? I have good news. They are in heaven. God looks at the heart not at the outward position or activities of a person. As humans, we see someone on drugs and alcohol or someone who committed suicide as being bad. God sees them as a scared little boy or girl whose heart was broken, so they used addictions to numb the pain. The Evil One tricked them and got them hooked on poison which killed them. The Evil One tricked them into ending their life. God blames the Evil One for their death. He doesn't blame you, and He doesn't blame them. God didn't take your child, the Evil One did. But here is the good news. Before your child died, in a split second, your child looked into Jesus' eyes of love and Jesus said, "If you want Me, I want you." No one can resist His eyes of love!

God has much for you to do on this side of heaven. As you follow God here on earth, you are building spiritual muscle so you can go to all the amazing places with your child in heaven.

You are not alone in this struggle. Your Daddy God in heaven is watching over you. He wants you to run to Him, so He can reveal His beautiful kaleidoscope through the broken pieces of your heart. I know you didn't want this kind of assignment, but our God is also the General in the army of heaven, and He has confidence in you! He sees that your DNA is made of faith, hope, and love.

He suffered so much, so that we could be reunited with our children. It's ok to cry with relief. Let all your worries about heaven and your child be released. Ask God to give you a confirmation or a sign that your child is safe and playing in heaven.

Crawl in your Daddy God's lap. Say this prayer out loud: "Daddy God, I was so shocked and embarrassed and confused that my child's life ended like this! Help me to get through all of this. Lift me above the floodwaters of confusion. (See Him lifting you and your family up.) Command all effects of shock and trauma to come out of my spirit, soul, and body. Use Your power to remove all confusion and to make me normal again in my body and soul. Rebuke the shadow of death and suicide around me and my family. I release all shame to You. Be the shade on my right hand, and don't let me feel stares and judgment. Help me to feel the truth that most good-hearted people have love and concern for me. I don't want to live in paranoia or be over-protective about my other children. Make the torment of fear dissolve under the power of Your love. Send the Comforter to wrap me in peace so I can finally rest. Fill me with Your joy which gives me strength."

Day **64**

WHEN GOD SAYS NO

Sometimes God says no to our requests no matter how loud we beg, promise, or curse. One reason He may say no is because He sees greater glory on the horizon. He sees forever, but we only see today. He is able to do far more abundantly **beyond** all that we ask or think, according to His power that works within us. (See Ephesians 3:20.) He will do "… things which eye has not seen and ear has not heard, and which have not entered the heart of man, for those who love Him" (1 Corinthians 2:9 NASB).

God is a gentleman, and He won't force Himself on anyone. In my life, He didn't do anything drastic unless He asked me first. As the pressure to take Tommy off of life support increased, I told God I wasn't **ever** going to give my permission. I could say no until hell froze over. I basically acted like a two-year-old and told God I was going to hold my breath as long as I had to. Three days later, I couldn't stand living on my own without God, so I relented and told Him the hardest thing I ever had to say: "Not my will, but Thy will be done." Mind you, I said that declaration kicking and screaming.

God has forever saved up for us. He is going to make up to us our loss with blessings beyond our wildest imagination. I know. I know. You didn't want treasure. You only wanted your beloved child. But God works in the unseen world. With your loss comes the advancement of God's Kingdom. Have faith in a big God. Hope in a good God. See His love in magnificent ways. He did not spare His own Son, how will He not give us all things that we need? (See 1 Corinthians 2:8-10.)

Dream big. What do you want God to do in the world to make it a better place? We asked God to make Osama Bin Laden a follower of Christ and you know what? I dreamed he has a grandson who did. I'll take that.

Say this "Prayer for Simple Faith" out loud: "Heavenly Father, I choose to trust You with a simple trust. I open the door wide to You! There are so many questions, but it doesn't matter, because **You** are the answer. I release all my fears to You. Any fear that is bound up in me, let it be loosed off of me. (Breathe out and in.) Give me abiding, consistent, living, faith that comes from my heart, not my head. I want to relax in my faith, which will bring a peace to my body and soul. Wrap me in Your counsel and correction. I don't want to grope in the darkness like a blind woman. Take my hand, and surround me and my family with the light of Your life."

CAMERON

L et me tell you about my precious and precocious nephew, Cameron David James. He was born on Tommy's birthday, two years earlier. On the day that Tommy was born, Cameron had a big birthday party with lots of gifts. He even got an electric tiny car. His mom, Suzie, asked him what he got for his birthday and he responded, "I got a baby cousin." Isn't it incredible that as a two-year-old, he wasn't thinking about material gifts? Cameron David James mirrors Tommy David James in some pretty unusual ways.

On the eve of Super Bowl Sunday, at age seven, Cameron started having severe headaches. The next day, Cameron was diagnosed as having a brain tumor, a glioblastoma multiform type four. His first surgery was scheduled so close to Valentine's Day (Tommy's heaven day), that I could hardly breathe. There I was, in a waiting room, down the hall from Tommy's last breath. Cameron's surgery was also on his father's 44th birthday. Cameron got forty-four stitches, of which he was very proud. He woke up from brain surgery wanting a mirror to see his stitches. On his second brain surgery, he asked the surgeon to make the stitches in a "U" shape so that his scars would say UT for the University of Texas. When he came out of surgery, he was in the same ICU room as Tommy had been. Cameron was in bed #27—Tommy's former bed. WOW!

The nurses called Cameron the bravest boy at TCH. He never flinched at giving blood or pricks of the finger. Once he had to pee in a cup, and in front of all the nurses, he **drank** his pee. The nurses flipped their flip charts and screamed their loudest screams. When the dust settled, Cameron revealed he had apple juice in his cup.

There are too many hilarious and amazing stories about Cameron for me to recount here. His short life would make a great movie. The following anecdote captures just one of these stories. Once, during his two years of treatment, Cameron read a bumper sticker that quoted an old song from the 80s. It said, "Don't worry. Be happy." Cameron said cheerfully, "That's me; I don't worry. I'm happy." Then his eyebrows wrinkled. "Well...except about the dying part." Then his eyes lit up with joy. "But then, I get happy when I think about seeing God and Jesus!" Wow! What faith! What courage! Years later, we named an eighth-grade Bible study in honor of his character: "Cameron's Courage."

Cameron and Tommy have the same middle and last names and the same birthday. Both had a heart-wrenching surgery near Valentine's Day, and they shared the same ICU bed. What an amazing tapestry God was weaving. Now we only see the bottom side of the tapestry not the glorious colorful side.

Cameron died almost two years after his first diagnosis. On the day that he died, I took my kids to say goodbye. We knew the time was close. Cameron was in a coma-like state, but I knew he would hear us. I wanted to make Cameron laugh, so I teased him by telling him in his ear that my daughter was going to marry his best friend and they would have a boy named Cameron. He couldn't talk, but his eyes started to flutter fabulously, and his mouth started to blow bubbles. He obviously was laughing on the inside and my girls saw it and were amazed. Then I told him to find Tommy and build me the biggest and best theater complex in heaven.

A week after Cameron died, his parents went to a Houston Astros professional baseball game and held up a sign for one of their star players: Mr. Craig Biggio. Craig had become good personal friends with Cameron and had even visited Cameron at home. The sign said, "Hit a home run for Cameron!" He did! The run secured a wildcard playoff spot, and the Astros would go on to win the National League pennant to advance to the World Series for the first time in franchise history!

Later that same year, Cameron's beloved University of Texas won college football's national championship—their first national championship in many years. Cameron saw the game on heaven's big screen with two million new friends. Many might call these sports events coincidental to Cameron's ordeal. I consider them to be part of the heavenly tapestry that I will one day get to enjoy in all of its brilliant, colorful, heavenly glory. One day, my Daddy God will put His loving arms around Suzie and me and explain the tapestry and all of its most intricately woven details. Until then, I am content to know that my Father in heaven holds all the keys of the Kingdom and all the mysteries of earth.

Is there a sports team that your child enjoyed on earth? You can ask God to show your child a big game in heaven! Remember to ask God to roll back the clouds and show the crowd cloud of many witnesses your family event. Your heavenly child **can** see all the happy events that you experience; they just see the events from a higher vantage point! Cameron is making plans to watch his sister's wedding!

MY STORY: AN ANGEL IS BORN

In the seventh month of my pregnancy, the ultrasound revealed a hypo-plastic left ventricle. The baby would need three open-heart surgeries over the course of his life to have even a 50 percent chance of survival.

On November 1st, Tommy David James screamed his head off when he was born. My best friend Cheryl was in the delivery room and from the strength of his cry she felt for sure the doctor had over-reacted to the ultrasound. "There's nothing wrong with that baby."

The nurses were great! They snuck our three kids (ages 6, 4, and 2), my parents, and my brother into the delivery room. It was a happy time for all of us. We took photos of all four of my children together. Little did anyone know, those were the only combined photos we would ever get to take. I will **forever** be indebted to those precious nurses at St. Luke's Hospital. Unfortunately, the doctor was right. He hadn't over-reacted; his diagnosis was accurate.

At five days old, Tommy was supposed to have his first open-heart surgery. But something was wrong. His body cavity filled up with liquid, and the surgery was cancelled. I got on KSBJ radio in Houston and asked the city to pray. Two days later, the doctor said, "He is as fit as I ever hoped he could be." The surgery was eight hours. A baby's heart is the size of its fist. Can you imagine operating on something so tiny? The hospital staff at Texas Children's Hospital was so courageous and full of faith that they performed two open-heart surgeries and two heart cauterizations. Still, Tommy did not improve. He had a ventilator and eighteen tubes and wires stuck into him every day of his life. The doctors were very perplexed by Tommy's sickness, but they never gave up with their faith which was exhibited through administering medical interventions.

When was your child born? What hospital was he born in? Was he born with a head full of thick, dark locks? I would love to see his or her baby pictures. Post it on my Facebook page *Mourning to Morning by Nancy James.*

THE DARKEST CLOUD

On December 11th, the doctors took Tom and I to a private counseling room. Today, I laugh because we must have looked like dumb, little lambs being led to the slaughter. We had no clue what was about to happen. They gently told us that during the second catheterization, performed earlier that morning, they had discovered Tommy's problem. His pulmonary arteries weren't large enough to sustain life. A transplant was not an option for us.

Tom threw his head on the table and sobbed. I was totally calm. "Don't worry this is just a minor setback." I don't know how; I know it sounds crazy, but I told the doctors, "I just know Tommy will live. I don't know how, but I know he will live." With that comment, the doctors were **sure** they had a sick little boy **and** a nut case mother on their hands.

On the figurative fortieth day, we went into our own wilderness. We cried, prayed, fasted, and believed for a miraculous new heart. I had several dreams that injected faith into me. I mailed

617 photos of Tommy all over the country and to sixteen other countries. One set of photos had his little penis sticking out! I imagined how mad he would be when he saw what I had done!

Believe it or not, home computers were just becoming popular and e-mail was brand new. Tom emailed daily updates about Tommy; it was our first exposure to e-mail and a real live reality show. Some people went on vacation and asked us to e-mail updates to their hotel receptionist. Teresa, a friend in Alabama, three states away, saw a picture of Tommy on her bulletin board! People were praying for Tommy in twelve countries and twenty-four states! Tom saw an angel in our bedroom one night. I heard an angel sing through our house. A nurse saw two angels at Tommy's bed, stroking his hair. I was crying and felt a strong, cool wind brush across me. I read the entire book of Psalms onto cassette tapes so that Tommy's spirit would be strengthened. I read Revelation to him, so if it was the Lord's will to take Tommy to heaven, he would be familiar with his new heavenly surroundings.

One morning I woke up at 8:50, and had the idea to connect the time to Luke 8:50. The verse said, "Don't be afraid. Just believe. She will live." I was convinced Tommy would live. But the curious thing is that neither my husband nor any trusted friends had any revelations. Now I know that those dreams were either from my mother's heart, desperate for a good word, or from my Father God to sustain me until the appointed time of Tommy's death.

These are but a few events of the James' Family Saga. Aren't you amazed at the sense of humor? It is real joy. The joy of the Lord is my strength. He will do the same miracle in you, if you ask Him. So ask.

I FELT LIKE I WAS LOSING MY MIND

The second hardest thing I've ever had to do is not being able to mother my child. I had to leave my baby at the sterile hospital with attendants who weren't me! My mothering hormones were still in high gear; no one thought to turn them off. I needed to breastfeed but there was no baby. I needed to hold him, care for him, love him...but I couldn't.

Once, I thought I was losing my mind. Our family was at the dinner table after we had purchased Tommy's casket earlier that day. During dinner, I felt like my mind was leaving through a hole in the top of my head. I chanted over and over under my breath, "I've got to have a baby. I've got to have a baby. I've got to have a baby," and I was rocking back and forth like a bag lady talking to her bag (no disrespect intended). My husband prayed a short prayer that whatever I was experiencing would stop—and it did!

We took the kids out on the driveway to rollerblade, and we let them stay up late even though it was a school night. My husband turned on the car headlights so they could see. We rejoiced with what we **did** have. We had three beautiful kids, and we relished them. It was as if we had made a toast with expensive champagne.

Overcome evil with good. Make a moment over a simple event, and enjoy it. Take your kids to do something fun every day. Take them to a park, a lake, an amusement park, the mall, an ice cream shop, or the movie theater!

OUR LITTLE VALENTINE

A week before Valentine's Day we decided that Tommy hadn't improved in a long time. We decided to stop the medical interventions and give God full reign to heal Tommy. It was this night that God gave me the dream that congratulated me for overcoming my fear of death. (See Chapter 34.) Since Tommy had a unique heart, there was no better day to take him off the tubes and wires than on Valentine's Day. Tom and I went to church with our family in the morning. We were glad it coincidentally fell on Sunday that year. During church, we could gain spiritual strength for our incredible day, and we could delay the dread. When we arrived at the hospital, we found Tommy's room had been decorated by Cupid's helpers. While we were at church, Tommy had been kept company by a host of "angels."

In his hospital room, we were surrounded by forty of our closest friends. CNN was at Tommy's hospital because a set of octuplets had been born. I was convinced God *coincidentally* had CNN at the hospital to report Tommy's miracle. I set up the tripod to capture it. We had communion with pretzels and lemonade, which were the only things I had available. I don't think God cared, do you?

A friend led our group in singing praise songs. There wasn't a dry eye in the room, except for mine. I was looking good; my hair looked like Maria Shriver's! My faith was reflected by my countenance and poise, but I was shaking like a leaf. This was the moment that we'd all been waiting for. It was the moment we would find out if our little guy would live or die. I could hardly stand the suspense, but I was sure I knew the answer. He would be going home with us!

PRAYING FOR RESURRECTION AND LIFE

After an hour, our guests left us with Tommy, the nurses, our pastors, and their wives. The nurses removed the wires and finally the ventilator. I was convinced that if Tommy could get free of the medical interventions, he would be just fine. Secretly, I blamed his problems on the interventions not on his faulty vein structure.

They handed my baby to me—my first hug since he was born. I put Tommy on my chest convinced that prayer and a mother's love would keep him alive. My sweet husband only got Tommy's hand wrapped around his finger. Tommy squeezed his finger so tightly like he had always done. We began speaking prayers of faith for him. I was getting excited because I could feel the Spirit of resurrection and life in the room. Then, within a few seconds, the grip was gone. I knew it because Tom started to cry. We kept praying and kept believing. Now was the time for resurrection to begin.

Our pastors prayed fervently, powerfully, and preciously. The words reminded me of Elijah's prayers. Then I put on my mother's hat and yelled at Tommy: "Tommy James, you get back in this body right now." Hey, I was desperate.

Meanwhile, the group of friends became a group of supporters. They gathered in a deserted hallway and continued singing. A security man invited them to an outside courtyard, which they did. They were right outside our window. At one point, I had considered buying balloons to be released if Tommy went to heaven, but I chose not to do it because I thought that planning a balloon release ahead of the fact would be admitting defeat.

POWER TEAM 2

After an hour of praying, the group of friends making up Team 1 left, and Power Team 2 came in to pray. Team 2 was a group of mighty prayer warrior women. I knew they would beat the gates of heaven and get Tommy back. They were like the wailing women of Africa; they prayed and prayed and prayed. They stroked my hair and rubbed my shoulders. It was a beautiful time. I was so proud to call them not just friends but sisters.

Four hours later, Tom and I walked out of his room. Arm in arm, each holding the other one up, we trudged down the hall. We looked so broken and yet so beautiful. We lost our hope, but we didn't lose each other. Tom described his condition from an old Indian painting by Fredrick Remington. The painting shows an Indian squaw who has found her dead husband on a battlefield, and she is desperately mourning her loss. The caption of the painting reads, "Her Heart Is on the Ground."

At home, Suzie, my sister-in-law, left presents for everyone including me. It was so sweet and creative. She left toys for the kids, a silver locket for me, and a children's book about heaven called *Let's Talk about Heaven* by Debby Anderson. We read this book to our kids at bedtime. I must have bought a zillion of those books and passed them out to friends. The book was good for us grown-ups too. I cherish my locket more than any possession I own.

Maybe you could order a locket online and put a picture of your cutie inside the locket, so you can wear them next to your heart. Or, you could buy a keychain that acts as a locket. Your child is one of the keys to your heart!

LEAVING FOR THE LAST TIME

The hardest thing I've ever done is walk away from my baby knowing I would never see him again. I remember walking out of Tommy's hospital room. It was the room my husband and I had visited every day for three-and-a-half months. As Tom and I walked out of his room, arm in arm, I had the thought, "Turn around and look at Tommy one last time."

"'What do you mean, 'one last time'?" I argued. I was coming back the next day like I always did. Then the **dark** reality hit me; this was my last time. This was my last trip to the hospital. I quickly turned around, gazed at Tommy, and blew him a kiss.

Then I had to walk away.

Oh, my gosh! A sword went into my heart. This couldn't be happening! I kept pushing myself down the hall. I kept telling myself, "Breathe. Just breathe." The hall, which was normally full of nurses, was oddly empty. They were understandably hiding. Who wants to witness two people saying goodbye to their child for the last time? I think they missed the most beautiful sight: two people arm in arm. We never looked so broken and yet so beautiful. Beautifully we held each other. Beautifully we walked down the lonely corridor together. It was our finest hour.

I don't think we were alone. I think there were angels lining the hallways and applauding as we trudged down the hall, whispering to one another, "Look at them still embracing, still trusting, still hoping for a miracle." I was convinced that we'd reach the end of the hall and hear a baby cry. It would be Tommy. Alas, it was not to be.

I am a hopeful romantic. I hope to meet those angels one day and to hear their side of the story. I believe that heaven records the finest moments of our lives. These moments aren't the times we scored a touchdown or doubled our portfolio; they are the acts of kindness that we do in secret, and all the moments we lived bravely when we could have given up. I hope to watch our celestial video of our finest hour together.

Day 73

ANGER IS A PRAYER

This is my favorite story about that fateful Valentine's Day. It was 8:00 p.m. and I was getting ready for bed. I felt weird; it was as if I were moving in slow motion. I brushed my teeth, put my pajamas on, and, in the pitch dark, walked to my side of the bed. Then, I heard a soft voice say, "Go on and hit Me. You know you want to." It was an invitation I'll never forget.

I grabbed my pillow and growled, "You're damn right I want to hit You!" And I began to hit the bedpost with all my might. I whipped it over and over. I pretended it was God. "I'm so f-ing mad at you! I'm so f-ing mad at you! I'm so f-ing mad at you!"

Then I dropped the pillow because, all of a sudden, I saw (in my mind) Jesus being tied to a post, but instead of the Romans whipping Him, I was! I saw how much He loved me when He so willingly gave me His back. It was Jesus who had said, "Go on and hit Me; you know that you want to." I am crying just remembering how much He showed me that He loved me that night.

Later, I would joke that on that night I used the "cuss word book" because I said every cuss word in every language and even made up a few new ones.

There is a powerful tool of healing. It's called **releasing.** I've mentioned this technique of releasing before, but I want to encourage you **not** to stop releasing. There's something so wonderful about releasing to the Great I Am in heaven. I release negative emotions everyday, not so much about Tommy, but about new stresses and pressures, worries and sorrows. I am crying now as I read this story, and I feel cleansed and renewed. You never get to the place of complete healing until you get to the pearly gates. Release, and take a deep breath. Breathe in life.

Say out loud the prayer from Chapter 58 again because it's perfect for today. "Lord of heaven, I need Your presence because You are the source of life and goodness. Refresh my spirit, soul, and body. Wash over me. Heal my heart and mind. By your authority, stop the compulsive thoughts that keep coming into my mind, or show me the root cause. I release my worries of _____. I release fears of _____. I release my bitterness tied to _____. You said to give You all my trouble. So I take this log off my shoulder, and I give it to You. Deliver me from all negative tendencies that I inherited from my family such as bitterness, worrying, or being fearful. I choose to lift up my eyes towards heaven, because my help comes from You, the maker of heaven and earth."

I'M SO MAD AT YOU!

I continued: "I'm so mad at You. You led me on. You let me think Tommy was going to live. I told the hospital such ridiculous statements of faith. How could You let this happen to me? I love You. During the first Passover, the idol worshippers lost a child, not the people that loved You!"

Then I struck the lowest blow I could think of. I yelled at the top of my lungs, "I HATE YOU!" (Not my finest hour.) Then I lay in bed staring at the ceiling. I listened with my heart and I felt something indescribable. A wonderful realization came over me. I did not hate God; I still loved Him. I was as mad as a hornet at the situation, but I still loved my Father God. What was my worst nightmare, losing a child or losing my faith? I passed the test! I did not lose my faith. Faith was more important than life.

That night, I slept better than I had ever slept in my life. It was a deep, deep, protective sleep. For a few seconds the next morning, my conscience hadn't connected with my memory, and I felt no pain. Then as my memory recalled the headline events, I felt sick and nauseous. But I could say, "I love You, God. I still do; I really do." I sounded like Sally Field at the Oscars, but in reverse.

As I thought of the tremendous sleep that I experienced, the proverb "Don't let the sun go down on your anger," came to my mind. (See Ephesians 4:26-28.)

Do you have trouble trusting God? Do you struggle with doubt and unbelief? This is a sign that you have underlying anger at God or someone who represented God. If you can forgive the person who gave you a bad impression of God, it is the first step to a new friendship with Him. He is waiting with an armful of love and He's wearing a raincoat for all the vomit you might spill on Him. He can take it, and He knows you need to unload. After you let it out, thank Him that He allows it, and that He still loves you. That is amazing grace!

Hold the Good Shepherd's hand, and say this "Prayer of Newness" to Him: "God, why do I have trouble trusting You? Who do I need to forgive? (He might bring a person to mind that wounded you.) I forgive _____ for hurting me and for giving me a wrong message about You. Disconnect me from this anger and all wrong messages I have believed about You. You hold the words and power that will heal me, and there is no one like You. I don't want to live alone, slugging through life. Dear Heavenly Father, I choose to "forgive You" for _____ and believe that You are good, kind, and faithful. You will never leave me. (In your mind's eye, let the Good Shepherd give you a new picture of Him with you so you have a true message about who He is.) In the meantime, I am looking forward to doing _____ with my child in heaven."

HOW TO GET MAD AT GOD

There is only one who can handle the anger that I hurl around, and that is God. I dump all my anger on God because He can take it. If I didn't have Him, I'd probably become a Lorena Bobbitt. When God watches me yell, I'm sure I provide His daily portion of chuckles. I am wondering; since your child's death, have you have gotten mad at God? It wasn't your fault. It seems all the coincidences went in the negative direction.

I highly recommend yelling out loud or at least writing your deepest feelings of disappointment. I know releasing your emotions in these ways can be a huge blessing. Yelling at God feels so good and it's cleansing. If you can find an open field, yell out loud really loud. If you can find a spiral notebook, fill it with your written thoughts.

I have said this several times before, but it is crucial! Always end a crying or a ranting session with positive words about faith and God's goodness. "Lie" if you must, but by the act of your will, say something faithful. I can't emphasize this prescription enough. End every crying session with a positive faith statement. Force yourself to give thanks for something especially if you do not feel like it.

Let your husband off the hook. Resist the urge to correct him, unless it is life threatening. Then say, "God, I don't know how, but I know You are going to turn all this pain to good. God, You will get me through this." Write a positive faith statement right here in this book.

If you are alone, scream, "I hate you! I release all my anger to You. I don't want to hold onto any of this anger. I give it all to You. (Breathe out and take a few minutes to release your emotion.) Thank You that You even allow me to be honest with You, and You won't abandon me."

IT IS GOOD

I t is good to have friends that love you. It's even better to have a church full of people that love you. Come feel the love.

I know it's a little awkward when everyone keeps saying, "I'm sorry." But that's ok. They are trying to show genuine love and care. You just have to respond with, "Thank you." In that moment, you are receiving their love. Love never fails. Love heals.

It is good to know that you don't have to have a stiff upper lip. You don't have to set a good example for others to follow. Several times, I fell prostrate on the ground crying my heart out at church. No one looked down on me. No one gave me stupid clichés. I felt loved.

It is good that the school and the church have memories of your child. They are good memories. A momentary sting and tears may accompany your first visits, but since your child spent some time there, it will be as if you are visiting him. You can ask the

God of heaven to send your child a postcard as you visit their school or establishment where they worked.

If someone offers "just let me know what I can do to help," have a list ready, and give them a few choices to pick from. Don't be bashful even if it's been two years since the funeral. If they offer, they want to help. Here are a few ideas in case you've forgotten: mow the lawn, pick up medicine, pick up milk and bread, frame a picture of your child, make a special book about your child. You can ask a teacher to write a story about your child and then save it in your special book.

MY HEART IS SO BROKEN

This is my second favorite story about my healing.

After Tommy's death, I went to church every Sunday challenging God: "My heart is so broken today that there is nothing You can do to fix it." But every Sunday, He miraculously healed my heart.

By the following Sunday, my heart would be in shreds again. I would challenge Him again. "Ok, You healed me last Sunday, but this Sunday is different. I am feeling worse than last Sunday." I truly was worse. Events such as receiving the death certificate, proofing the headstone, seeing babies, and missing milestones all made me feel worse.

Do you know what? God healed my heart each Sunday. I remember a lady complimenting me: "I can't believe you're at church already." My thought was, *Where the hell else would I go to ease pain like this? Dinner and a movie?*

Today, I'm the woman standing on her chair in exuberant praise during a worship service. I've even thought to myself, I bet *Tim and Mel think that I am crazy. If they only knew. I am crazy.* I am crazy in love with God, who kept me from going crazy. He rescued me from the pit of depression.

I mentioned this before, but if you don't have a church home or a support group, google *House of Prayer*. Jesus said, "My house will be called a house of prayer" (Matthew 21:14 NIV). Your church should feel like home. It should be full of friendly people who want to be there out of love. Heck! I wish you could come to my church! Once you find one, if you feel a little awkward, just sit in the back. Trust me; the music will soothe your soul. It will be amazing! You might cry, but it will be such a good release. Sometimes, if I cried at church, I didn't have to cry all week!

Day 78

SPINNING THE WHEEL OF FORTUNE

In the midst of Tommy tottering between life and death, I desperately wanted to know if he would live or die. I read the Bible like a beggar woman looking for food. I clawed at the word. "Speak to me about Tommy." I spun open my Bible like I was spinning the wheel of fortune.

Once during Tommy's ordeal, I awoke to see the time on the clock was 9:24. I looked up every verse that matched the response I wanted. I found Matthew 9:24 that said, "The child will not die but live." There was my sign! I found a scripture to support my position. I found a scripture that promised a miracle.

After Tommy died, I couldn't read the Bible for a long time. It hurt me to read it. I saw so many "promises" that hadn't been fulfilled (yet). I knew my Father had the words of eternal life, but I had to **fight** to believe that truth. In the last few days, something important dawned on me. He said He would never leave me or forsake me. (See Hebrews 13:5.) He didn't! He was with me even on the day that Tommy went to heaven. He was there! Trust me!

If there wasn't a God, or if He had left me, I would be a crazy lady eating green caterpillars right now!

Today, I believe God's words in His book are alive and active. I can't predict what the awesome and mysterious God is going to do. In the beginning, I prioritized what God was going to do above who He is and understandably so. My son's life was in limbo, but my faith was in limbo too. God's Word is the bread of life not a Chinese fortune cookie!

Have you read any psalms from the Bible? Pick one of the psalms below, and read it today. Change the word "enemy" into whatever you are battling like fear, depression, or hopelessness.

Psalm 23, 34, 43, 46, 56, 61, 62, 63, 70, 71, 77, 84, 86, 91, 95, 97, 100.

STAY AWAY FROM CRYSTAL BALLS

Speaking of fortune, don't go to a fortuneteller. The one true God doesn't communicate through crystal balls. He will speak to you Himself. His voice will be kind and gentle. He will speak to you through His book—the Bible. There are a lot of spirits in the world. The only spirit you want to talk to or listen to is the **Holy** Spirit.

My understanding of your hurt and confusion is only a grain of sand compared to all the beaches of the earth. Our Father owns all those beaches, and He knows the number of grains of sand on each and every one! His wisdom is equivalent to all the grains of sand in the world. His answers are like the waves that wash upon the beach. Wave by wave, His answers come. Little by little, His healing comes.

---

[3] **Kona Life Church**; Pastor Damien Wong. 75-5699 Alii Drive. Kona, HI 96740. (808) 326-7000. KonaLifeChurch.org.

Believe in the God of your childhood again. He is good, kind, and faithful. He might not look very faithful right now. From our perspective, He looked like He was absent. But He is desperate to tell you something that changes everything. Look into your Father's heart. What do you see?

Say this out loud: "Lord, establish Your presence in me, and let Your presence bring peace to my spirit, soul, and body. Lord, help me to trust You even in hard times. Help me to trust You when I don't see or understand the plan. Let me not rely on my own strength and the arm of the flesh but on Your ability and power. Lord grant rest to my soul. Lord, I receive the anointing of life to overcome the works of death and destruction in my life. I receive the goodness of Your glory. Today, I will factor the power of God into my life. Holy Spirit, activate the supernatural in my life. Give me revelation of Your truth and let this bring freedom to my spirit, soul, and body." Pray this for each member of your family too.

I got this prayer from the Facebook page of Kona Life Church in Kona, Hawaii, by Pastor Damien Wong. Check out their website too. (Thanks Debbie!)

BITTERNESS

On Valentine's Day, exactly one year after Tommy's departure, I totaled our family car. I hit the nicest eighty-year-old lady in Houston. By the time the ambulance arrived to put her on the stretcher, we were hugging like sisters.

The day began as an ordinary trip to the grocery store. My mind was completely distracted by a situation that I was furious over. I stopped at a busy intersection and decided not to cross the street until it was empty. I looked once; I looked twice; it was clear. Then POW! I was hit. I never saw it coming. After I crawled out from under the airbag, I dreaded meeting the driver because the accident was my fault. I knew they would be furious. When I met the driver (Aileen), she was the sweetest grandmother in the world. Instead of yelling at me, she let her love flow all over me.

I can't explain why, but there was an instant connection between us. Aileen and I were hugging and making polite conversation. In fact, the wrecker guy looked at us with amazement. He finally asked, "Do ya'll know each other?" We looked at each other and said, "Well, we're sort of sisters." We were sisters—sisters in the Spirit. God chose Aileen for a reason. She could have been furious with me; instead, she reached out in love. Her love threw ice cold water on my red-hot rage.

I wrote this book so that you wouldn't be spiraling out of control like I was. You've been through a big trauma, so if you find yourself out of control with rage or sadness, ask your Father God to pour His perfect love into you. Then overcome evil with good. Like Aileen, go and pour your love on someone. Rage and sadness will dissolve out of your soul.

Put on some music. Hold God's hand and say this out loud: "Lord God, I choose to receive Your grace and mercy. (Take several deep breaths.) Show me where I am carrying anger and bitterness. (Wait for Him to show you.) I release this anger about _____ to You right now. I don't want to spiral out of control. Hold me tightly. Wrap me in forgiveness, and lead me in Your goodness. Release Your glory. Lead me in Your love forevermore. Heavenly Father, impart Your resurrection life into my innermost being. Deposit Your hope into the core of my being. Plant the seed of Your perfect love into every cell of my spirit, soul, and body, and make it grow in exponential ways."

NOTHING IS AN ACCIDENT

I knew that having a car accident on Valentine's Day, exactly a year after Tommy died, was no accident. I knew that my loving Daddy God was trying to get my attention. He had tried on numerous occasions, but I wasn't listening. So, He had to resort to a drastic measure to save me from destroying myself and my family. He said He would never leave me or forsake me. He was right! He stepped in.

Have you ever had a coincidence, which was so special that it seemed like God was in it? A divine appointment is a meeting which was inspired and God-led. God is sovereign; He is all-knowing and all-powerful. My "accident" with Aileen was a divine appointment. Let me tell you her side of the story.

Aileen had stopped driving a long time ago. She let her niece drive her around town. On the day of the accident, her niece was busy. Aileen drove on a street that she usually avoided because it is often busy. For some reason she felt an urge to drive down the street where we collided. She was also driving in the rain which she ordinarily would never drive in!

I believe that my Father sovereignly set up the driver, the location, and the day so that it was no accident. I believe He chose Aileen as His vessel of love for me. I needed a sweet little "Nana" or "Gigi" to love me and to tell me everything was going to be all right. (I am crying so hard as I remember her. I didn't realize until today the depth of what her purpose was for me.)

I was able to bless Aileen by telling her my story of how God used her to knock some sense into me by forcing me to confront and get rid of my bitterness. She was so humble and appreciative. Today, she is playing with Tommy and Cameron. I will ask God to introduce her to your child in heaven.

I want to hold you, stroke your hair, and tell you that everything is going to be all right. I want you to know that life feels like it is spinning out of control, but your Father has a plan and a purpose. He will never leave you, forsake you, disown you, cast you aside, or wash His hands of you.

There are no coincidences with God. In fact, it's a good thing to pray every day that God will bring a divine appointment to your kids (and yourself). Sometimes kids can't hear something from us (like when I wasn't listening to God!), but they will receive it from a stranger. It is amazing, sister. (Thanks Glenda!)

I WAS THE WRECK

The car accident was a reality check that revealed a lot of problems inside my heart. I needed an overhaul or an attitude adjustment. My issues were rage, impatience, and arrogance. I didn't make excuses. I aggressively dealt with my issues on three levels: spiritually, practically, and medically.

Spiritually, I asked my Father to forgive my bitterness, and I asked my family to forgive me. My words and thoughts were bitter which mirrored a bitter heart. Every day, I asked for a new heart. I had a contaminated heart that was polluting my life.

Also, I was both arrogant and ignorant to think that I was the only one who'd suffered a loss. The truth is that most people have lived their own tragedy-to-triumph story. I was the one being hollow. I asked my Father to forgive me and to remove all traces of arrogance. There are only two people at a pity party: you and the devil.

Practically, I resisted any impulse to be bitter or arrogant. I lived in a world that played by certain rules. I couldn't expect the world to change just for me.

Medically, I realized that the rage was not normal. I got anti-depressants for a few years.

How are you acting differently? You cannot go through a major trauma and come out unscathed. Ask for an honest opinion from a busybody; they'll tell you the truth. From anyone else do not accept, "You're fine." They are lying.

I love you enough to tell you that you **will** have issues because you are human. Hurting people hurt people. Deal with your issues so you won't hurt your family and others in your sphere of influence! Seek professional and spiritual help. Don't make excuses for yourself or ignore issues. Consider addressing the issues as an appointment for a "spiritual spa."

Take the Good Shepherd's hand and pray: "I had a new sadness hit me today. (Breathe out.) Lord, I release this sadness to You. I release hopelessness to You. Hold me tight! Establish my family in Your love. Pump Your resurrection life into my family and fill us with Your peace that passes my understanding. Infuse hope into the cells of my spirit, soul, and body. Fill me with the force of Your life. Heal me inside out. Make all of my disorders be dissolved by Your love."

HOW TO BREAK STRONGHOLDS

If you don't deal with your issues, they will come out in your tissues and into issues of your family! I have been honest about my anger at God. It is not right to be angry at God, but it is normal and He loves us anyway. God **hates** anger and bitterness because of the pain and trauma it causes us and those around us. My anger was spreading like wildfire to my family. I was even mouthing off to the Wal-Mart attendant. Come on! Who can mouth off to them? They are so sweet and adorable! God allowed the car wreck to get my attention.

Let all bitterness, indignation, wrath (rage, bad temper), resentment (anger, animosity), quarreling (brawling, clamor, contention), and slander be banished from you, with all malice (spite, ill will, or baseness of any kind). Forgive just as He forgives you. (See Ephesians 4:31.)

"For wherever there is jealousy and selfish ambition, there you will find disorder and evil of every kind" (James 3:16 NLT)

Work at living in peace with everyone…for those who are not holy will not see the Lord. Look after each other so that none of you fails to receive the grace of God. Watch out that no poisonous root of bitterness grows up to trouble you, corrupting many" (Hebrews 12:14-16 NLT).

As your sister who dearly loves you, let me tell you that bitterness is a snake in the grass. Your bitterness will creep onto your family and poison them! Our Good Shepherd warns us that we won't see Him in heaven if we allow bitterness to consume our lives. Wow! Now that is a motivator!

#1 – Ask forgiveness for yourself. When we are wounded, we wound in return. Tell God you are sorry for your anger and bitterness. Repentance brings times of refreshing from God! (See Acts 3:19.)

#2 – Forgive others. Who are you frustrated or angry at? Make a list. Ask God for His supersonic rocket fuel of forgiveness. You can't do it on your own. God doesn't blame you, and He doesn't want you to blame yourself or others. Blame and regret keep you chained to the past.

#3 – Bless them. Jesus said to repent, forgive, **and** bless your enemies. There are cycles and patterns of pain and destruction that repeat in each generation. Repenting, forgiving, **and** blessing your enemies breaks the **stronghold** for your children and future generations. I know it's hard, but blessing your enemies is the door to happiness. (See Matthew 5:44.)

#4 – Take His hand and say this out loud: "Father God, open the windows of my soul and let Your light of life blow through my soul. Do some house cleaning! Blow on me, God. Touch me and give me Your courage to do this! Forgive me for pride, anger, and judgment. I renounce them. I forgive the drunk driver, insurance companies, doctors that I felt could have done more, my boss, my husband, my child for _____ (drinking on the night he died, etc.), and the church. I "forgive" You, God, and I forgive myself. I release blame out of my spirit, soul, and body. Father, get rid of any trace of self-blame. You have to do it. (Squeeze the Good Shepherd's hand.) I bless my enemies and their families, businesses, and lives. Heavenly Father, disconnect me and my family from all negative and wrong tendencies we inherited from our ancestral lineage. Superimpose Your perfect DNA on my family so we can carry out Your destiny on the earth without any hindrances. Fill my parched heart with your Holy liquefying presence. Open a valve in my spirit, soul, and body to release all the stress and pressure that I am carrying. Fill my entire being with Your power, love, and sound mind." (Picture yourself filling up.)

Dear friend, remember to ask forgiveness for yourself. Forgive others, and bless your enemies like your life depends on it... because it does. You are staking a claim for a healed life, for a better life, for a new life. You are not alone; you have the Good Shepherd beside you.

September 10, 2001

I want to share a story that highlights that all things are under God's rule and control, and that nothing happens without His knowledge or permission. All things go through His hands. You will see His mercy in the midst of chaos.

On September 10, 2001, I was having coffee with three good friends. We were at a new coffee shop called *Starbucks*. I noticed that one of my friends looked gray and scared. She finally told us a secret. She revealed that for several days, she had recurring dreams where she was kidnapped and killed by a knife. She said, "The weirdest thing is that in the dream, I am not scared, and I feel no pain." Her confession reminded another friend about a similar type of dream.

Teresa had dreamed for several nights that she and her child were in a car and an 18-wheeler purposely rammed into them, pushing them off a high freeway overpass. "But," she said, "I was not afraid. We felt no pain because we didn't hit the ground;

we suddenly soared up to heaven, and I saw the most beautiful colors that are not even on earth!"

This prompted the third friend to remember a dream where she was in her house when it caught fire. She was also not afraid. She lay down and went to sleep. When she awoke she heard the most heavenly music. It was incredible, indescribable music. This reminded me of my dream!

I was kidnapped along with many others. We all had our cell phones, and I told everyone, "Call home. Don't worry about the kidnappers. Just do it!" In the dream, I was near West Street, which was the site of the next day's events.

The next day revealed the horror in our nation. As the day progressed, my friends and I called each other. Each of us had dreamed a piece of that day! God was not shocked by the events. **He was standing in the middle of everything**. He was in the tower. He was on the airplane. He was at the pentagon. The theme of our dreams was that no one felt pain or fear. Why? Because He was holding their hands. He was mercy in the midst of chaos.

If your child died suddenly in an accident, the Good Shepherd was there. Your child wasn't alone, didn't feel pain, didn't experience fear. Why? Because He was holding their hand. He took them to eternity. In a split second, they were seeing colors they had never seen before. They heard majestic music they had never heard before.

In a moment, they were home and at peace in the palace of the Prince of Peace. The Prince is the door to a glorious infinity. He welcomes everyone who welcomes Him. He is no stranger to suffering. He was rejected, tortured, and left alone. Like a rose, He was trampled on the ground, but unlike anyone else who has suffered, He willingly, joyfully took the suffering because He knew it was the only way He could ransom us from a sinful world.

Let us fix our eyes on Jesus, the leader and source of our faith. For the joy set before Him, He endured the cross and its shame and agony, and sat down at the right hand of the throne of God. (See Hebrews 12:2.) We can't understand all the decisions of an awesome God, but He is well acquainted with our pain. He has suffered more than we have. Bring your pain to Him, and let Him carry it. He is all you will ever need.

Close your eyes, and ask the Good Shepherd to show you what He was doing when your child died. When I asked that question, He showed me that He was standing behind me. He took Tommy in His arms and lovingly admired him. Then He passed Tommy to an angel, and He stayed to comfort me. I even saw Him massaging my shoulders. I always had neck problems, but not after that day!

HOW MUCH ARE YOU WORTH?

I know you look around at all the people who do not have a child in heaven, and you feel sad, bewildered, and abandoned. I know that you don't feel very valued by your Heavenly Father right now, but that is going to change. You may even feel like the step-child. I know how you feel. I even started to have lower back pain as if I had been stabbed in the back. The truth is, you have a child that went to heaven, but it's not true that you are loved less by our Heavenly Father. You **have** to believe those unworthy feelings are not true. He loves you with an everlasting love that reaches past Pluto! You are His dear child that He wants to wrap in His big, strong arms. Did you know your Heavenly Father has numbered the hairs on your head? Wow!

"Are not two sparrows sold for a farthing? and one of them shall not fall on the ground without your Father [knowing it]" (Matthew 10:29 KJV, brackets mine). Think of it, not one of these little brown sparrows that are caroling forth their praises to God will fall to the ground without the notice of the Heavenly Father. Not one of those little brown sparrows drops to the ground but

His eye marks its fall. "But the very hairs of your head are all numbered" (Matthew 10:30 KJV). If God cares for a sparrow that has no soul, how will He not care for one soul purchased by the blood of Christ? One soul is worth more than all the world. For one soul, Jesus would have passed through the agony of Calvary that that one might be saved in His kingdom. "Fear ye not therefore, ye are of more value than many sparrows" {Matthew 10:31 KJV).

When our little "sparrows dropped to the ground," rest assured; His eye marked the spot where they fell. Our Heavenly Father was holding our children in His hands as they went from this life to the next. Did you catch the part that Jesus would go through the torture, shame, and agony of the cross just for you? Dear one, that means He did all that **just** so we could be reunited with our children. Wow! Swallow that truth down to your gut!

How much are you worth? Here is the Hollywood movie's version. You were the reason the handsome Prince suffered and died, so He could rescue you from the evil one. If He had stayed in His heavenly castle, you would be in the dungeon of the evil one for all eternity, being tortured. Instead, the handsome Prince asked His Father, the King, if He could give His life to ransom you. The King said, "Yes! I have had my eye on her since the moment she was born. Go at once, for she would make a wonderful bride for you and a daughter-in-love for me."

FEELING BETRAYED BY GOD

When Tommy died, I felt like God had abandoned me at the altar and had run off with my best friend. Therapists have discovered that feeling betrayed shows up in the lower back as throbbing pain. (And you thought you just bent down wrong!) The body will often mirror what is going on in the soul. When I discovered this interesting anomaly, I ask my sister Debbie to administer special healing prayer. For the first time in twelve years, my lower back pain left for good! As your big sister of faith, I am going to dedicate a lengthy prayer on this so that you don't have to carry it for twelve years like I did! This prayer will work for **any** betrayal from a loved one.

Let's hold His hand and gently pull that knife out. Get a tissue box. You really need to cry for this one. Watch a sad movie, crawl into your Heavenly Father's lap, and say these words: "Daddy, I need Your help to remove this excruciating pain that is my heart and back. Send Your angels to help me. I renounce all feelings related to betrayal out of my spirit, soul, and body. Help me, Lord, if I leave anything out. I release all hurt, all betrayal, all shock, all worthlessness, all inferiority, all bewilderment, and all confusion out of my soul and body. I choose to believe that I have Your undivided attention and love. I also release all envy, all jealousy, and all bitterness about _____ to You right now that is related to friends that still have their children. Wash that junk out of me as I wash my soul with my tears. I release and let go of feeling unloved, forgotten, abandoned, and rejected. I release feeling like an orphan to You, Heavenly Father. If I picked up any self-pity or martyr-likeness along the way, I give that to You too. I don't want this junk anymore. I don't want to live like this anymore. I renounce and disconnect from all these false feelings. I throw them on the ground! I step on them now! Heavenly Father, take all this stuff **away** from me and throw it in the pit."

(In your mind's eye, I want you to picture this next part. Get elaborate in your vision. I have a friend that went to her closet and literally put on these clothes!) "Heavenly Father, I have dried my eyes and with conviction in my heart, I have decided to put on these new clothes instead. I choose to put on Your blouse of loveliness, the vest of worthiness, the skirt of faithfulness, the necklace of redemption, the scarf of contentment, and the earrings of acceptance. One earring is Your acceptance of me, and the other is acceptance of myself. To all of these things I add the belt of truth, to tie everything together. No outfit would be complete without the sandals of assurance that say, 'I am Your beloved daughter.' If You are a King, that makes me a princess! Wow! Heavenly Father, thank You for loving me unconditionally. Thank You for adopting me into Your family. Thank You for truly caring about me and my family. I **love** You!" It's time to go out to dinner and celebrate! You can even "put on your new garments of praise." (See Isaiah 61:3.)

WHO WILL LOVE THE KING?

It had been almost two years since Tommy died, and I still felt heart broken. I wasn't broken over losing Tommy; I was heart-broken over losing my Father. Why had my Heavenly Father abandoned me at my most desperate moment?

This confusion left my heart tattered and torn. As I sensed my heart becoming hard, I began to entreat my Father to explain His decision lest I become a brittle and bitter young woman. My question boiled down to one statement: "I trusted You, and You abandoned me. I feel as if You left me at the altar and married my best friend!"

Then the answer came to me while I was reading on an airplane. The trip was an attempt to celebrate our tenth wedding anniversary, but I was just going through the motions. I was not very joyful. Suddenly, a revelation jumped off the page and hit me square in the eyes. I pray a similar revelation hits you in the same way.

Wealth adds many friends,
But a poor man is separated from his friend.

Many will seek the favor of a generous man,
And every man is a friend to him who gives gifts.

All the brothers of a poor man hate him;
How much more do his friends abandon him!
He pursues *them with* words, *but* they are gone.

He who gets wisdom loves his own soul;
He who keeps understanding will find good.
(Proverbs 19:4-8 NASB)

I interpreted the passage to mean that my Father God is the Great King and has many children and subjects. Most of His children love and honor Him only because He is generous. So, actually the King is a poor man because He has no one who really loves Him for who He is; people only love Him for His money and gifts.

I never thought about my Father God as not having real love. He created love and is love; yet, most of us only love Him because of His generous gifts. I felt so sad for Him. Then, the light bulb popped on! What if He denies a gift to one of His children, and the child chooses to love Him anyway? They choose to trust Him in spite of the circumstance. Then the King, the Father, has finally found true love! The child has also found true love because he or she has chosen the higher road—the road less traveled.

I am crying right now as I write this. For so long I was mad at God for not loving me "the way I deserved," and yet, all along, it was I who had little love. Let this idea cleanse your soul, and let it mesh your heart into His. Let it wash away all your hurt and confusion.

Remember God loves you more in a moment than anyone could in a lifetime.

Day **88**

ON THAT DAY

You, your husband, and your children will walk down the streets of heaven as in a parade. You will be holding each other's hands and a blue sash will be draped across each of you. Your beloved child will be walking beside you.

On that day Holy to the Lord will be inscribed on the sash. As you approach the Great Throne Room, the King of heaven will greet you. He will embrace you and say "Welcome." Then He will turn you toward the crowd and introduce you. He will say, "These are my beloved friends; welcome them, as I welcomed you. They have been faithful when others have fallen. They have been hopeful when all hope appeared gone. They have loved when others have hated. Let the celebrations begin! Well done, My faithful friends! Receive your reward!"

Can you picture this event? Watch the movie, *The Chronicles of Narnia: The Lion, the Witch and the Wardrobe*. At the very end of the movie there is a scene like the one above. Pretend you and your family are being congratulated. Watch the movie and hear the crowd cheering. See the streamers swirling. Feel the King's joy and pride over your family. Then hear His voice booming over the crowd! His voice is mightier than the sound of a thousand mighty water falls. His voice is powerful and yet peaceful at the same time.

REGRET AND UNRESOLVED ISSUES

D o you have any regrets? Did you get to say good bye? Do you have unresolved issues with your child? I have good news! With God, all things are possible. He is a good Father. You can do all of the above by writing it out! Have a box of tissues handy. I would do this with your spouse or a good friend. You can also help your other children write a goodbye letter or draw a picture. This is a wonderful way to bring closure. I hate the word closure because actually there can be an ongoing conversation between you and God. You can't talk to your child, but God can give your child your messages and videos!

Deal with your regrets or they will keep you chained to the pain of the past. Regret will cause you to relive your child's death over and over. "I wish I hadn't let them go out that night." "I wish I had said, no." Dear one, what happened with your child is so much bigger than you. You could not have stopped anything. I had a baby with a flawed heart. Down the hall was a lady who delivered eight babies with eight perfectly formed hearts. Release yourself from any regret.

Forgive your child: In doing so, you are cutting off the ghost of regret and remorse. Forgive your child for any error that resulted in their death. They didn't mean to do it. They didn't understand all the pain they would cause. They were just being kids.

Crawl in your Daddy God's lap. Pray this "Prayer of Closure": "God You are so wonderful! You are better than I ever imagined. My whole life I was afraid of You, and now at the worst time in my life, I discover that You are good, kind, and faithful. Lift me up to Your throne room. I give You all the regrets I have related to my child's death. (See yourself giving Him your regrets.) Heal me through and through. Heavenly Father, stop the train of thoughts with the power of Your peace. Touch my kids. Keep them out of trouble. Give them divine appointments with people who will lead them to a closer walk with You. Tell my child in heaven that I miss them and that I am sending them a letter. Tell them that I am not mad anymore. Tell them that I totally and completely forgive them! Tell them to enjoy their new life and build me a _____. Thank You for completely loving me, faults and all. I love You, Lord. I love You. I love You."

BE YOURSELF—
HEALING IS HERE

God has brought me to a great place of intimacy with Him as He has begun to release a continual healing into my life. As I admit my anger and sorrow and run to Him for help, He picks me up, puts me on His lap, and loves me through it all. He never lets me go.

My great desire for writing this book is to demonstrate the truth that you can totally be yourself with God, no matter if you are sad, angry, or simply ok. He understands our brokenness and grief, and He loves us where we are. Jesus is the accurate picture of God. He said, "If God were your Father, you would love Me, for I proceeded forth and have come from God, for I have not even come on My own initiative, but He sent Me" (John 8:42 NASB).

Print this prayer. Pray it everyday even if you only have energy to whisper.

Dear Lord,

I release to You all my pain, all my grief, and all my sorrow and confusion. I release it new every day. Let it float out of me like balloons. I send it all to You.

I release any regrets, any blame, any shame to You. Wash Your love over me.

Give me Your wisdom and strength to keep the faith in You and Your goodness.

Shine Your Light on me. Drive away the darkness I feel. Don't let the spirit of heaviness consume me.

Fill me with faith in You, hope in future, and love for myself, others, and especially, You, God.

Hold me when I cry. I hold You in one hand, and when sadness comes, I will cry with You because You will not let me break into a zillion little pieces.

Reveal Your perfect plan for me and my family. Fill me with Your courage, Your wisdom, and knowledge to accomplish all that You want me to do.

Give me eyes to see, ears to hear, and a heart to perceive Your love and truth.

I declare, God, You will give me a good life here on this earth if I keep following You.

Thank You for adopting me into Your kingdom and family. I gladly accept being Your daughter, which is crazy because that means I am a princess!

God's love is meteoric,
    his loyalty astronomic,
His purpose titanic,
    his verdicts oceanic.
Yet in his largeness
    nothing gets lost;
Not a man, not a mouse,
    slips through the cracks.
How exquisite your love, O God!
    How eager we are to run under your wings,
To eat our fill at the banquet you spread
    as you fill our tankards with Eden spring water.
You're a fountain of cascading light,
    and you open our eyes to light. (Psalm 36:5-9 MSG)

Delight yourself in the Lord;
And He will give you the desires of your heart.

Commit your way to the Lord,
Trust also in Him, and He will do it. (Psalm 37:4-5 NASB)

64 PRESCRIPTIONS FOR HEALING

1.   Plant a flower garden and give it a special name to remember your cutie. We set aside a small area in our yard and called it our "Valentine Garden." The plants have red and white flowers. One tree has heart shaped leaves and another tree buds around Valentine's Day. One plant is called *Angel's Wing*.

2.   Have your ears pierced. Here's the analogy. When your child died, the Good Shepherd allowed a piercing of your heart. That piercing brought pain, but if you keep your eyes on God, the pain will be momentary. The earrings represent the beauty that God will make come out of your pain, and out of the pain, God will make many beautiful things.

3.   As you keep your eyes and heart on God, you will walk in true wholeness rather than false happiness.

4.   The closer you abide with your Heavenly Father, the more the emptiness without your child will dissipate.

5.   Share your healing moments with your family, kids, and grandparents. They need helpful advice too. Send a quick little e-mail: "I was dreading their birthday, but I decided that on their birthday, we will go to a fun place with the kids. You are welcome to join us."

6. It's ok to use activities as anesthesia as long as you know that true healing comes from doing those activities **with** your Heavenly Father. Actively practice engaging the presence of God by doing your favorite things **with** the Lord. Go shopping, watch TV, read a magazine, watch baseball, paint a room, cook a recipe, decorate a room. Find something restful to do and picture the Lord with you. If you can afford it, take your kids to Disney World, even if it's for three days. Find a time when Disney is running a special.

7. Get a maid or someone to help clean your house.

8. Watch comedy movies and funny TV shows.

9. Take care of your spouse sexually. To state the obvious, men need sex. Even in crisis situations, men need sex. It's not their fault that they desire sex, our Heavenly Father made them that way. He knew the human race would need one gender to keep sex going, or the first tragedy would cause both genders to isolate themselves and thereby end the human race. Besides its immediate pleasurable sensations, sex helps both partners process sorrow and endure grief. Why sex? As your husband heals, he can be there to help you. Sex will heal you in the deep places in the core of your being. It will be cleansing. It will help to push out the pain.

10. Give yourself permission to splurge on yourself. Don't feel guilty. Go to the movies, spa, and on trips. Invite a friend to go with you, but don't go into debt!

11.   Find an email buddy. It feels good to click "Send Mail." Call it "sending your SOS." Sometimes you will literally drag yourself to the computer because you will be bent over in depression and confusion. Write a short request for prayer. As soon as you click "Send Mail," you will feel a million times better. Go figure! You can go to my Facebook for Mourning to Morning. Follow it so we can help each other. Tell me how you are feeling. Tell me things that helped you from the book. Share your ideas of healing.

12.   Keep your prayers simple! Prayers should reflect your feelings such as anger, hurt, and confusion. You need to daily sit still and have a releasing time. Picture yourself releasing the negative emotions to your Heavenly Father.

13.   Always, always, always end a prayer, especially an angry prayer, with a positive statement about God. Even if it is, "No matter what, I am going to trust You, Lord."

14.   Listen to the messages in your head. Accept the positive and renounce the negative such as, *I'll never enjoy Christmas without my child.* Instead, take that message and make it, *Christmas will be different, but with God, I will enjoy it!* You may want to write it and put it out for your family to read. They are struggling too.

15.   When you feel increasingly depressed, it is a signal from your body telling you to sit down before the Lord and release all the negative emotions out of your body and onto the Prince of Peace. He died on the cross to take all your pain and sorrow. He's dying for you to do it! Make a notecard reminding yourself to set aside releasing time.

16. If you are sad about something specific, don't go to bed without giving it to your Heavenly Father. Tell Him how you feel even if it's one sentence. Ask Him to make you feel better. Always end with a positive statement of hope.

17. Try to eat regularly: three meals with light snacks in between. Do it for your kids too. If friends invite you to lunch, go! Do it as a love gift for them; they are doing all they know to help you.

18. Go to bed early. I fought this prescription for a long time. This new season of early-to-bed won't last forever, but it may last for several years.

19. If you exercised in the past, try to resume it. Give yourself permission to be casual about it. Walk the dog. Use it as a time to pray, cry, and praise.

20. I love to cry around my dogs. They would "sniff" that something was wrong and they'd quickly jump in my lap and lick me! Their love comforted me. If you have a dog, you know what I am talking about. If you don't have a dog, get one! It's a scientific fact that dogs bring healing. We adopted a cat that had foster parents, so we knew the exact personality of the cat we were adopting. She is the most loving, cuddly, talkative cat on the planet! She's just perfect for us!

21. During the day, stop long enough to notice the good things that are happening. Often these are little things. Thank You, Lord, for a dishwasher. *Thank You, Lord, for AC in 105°F weather. Thank You for kids who are loud*

and messy. I verbalized quick arrow prayers of thanks. Keep an "Oprah" grateful journal in your head!

22. Repeat these words to yourself daily: "Life is good because God is with me." "I love my life." "The joy of the Lord is my strength."

23. Don't avoid a crying session by forcing yourself to focus on the good. I usually focused on the goodness of God and my life **after** a necessary grieving time. Just remember to picture yourself **with** the Lord while you are crying. It keeps the men in the white jackets from showing up at your house, and it shortens the crying session.

24. Most importantly, while you are crying, hold on to Jesus for dear life. Let Him pull you through the grieving time. Let Him pull you through the process like He would pull thread through the eye of a needle. You are the thread, and He is the needle. He is making something beautiful of your family's life.

25. If you hold sorrow in one hand and Jesus in the other, the crying session won't last as long. Go figure! Many times the phone rang or something interrupted me. This happened so many times that I began to trust the interruptions as God's way of telling me, "Everything will be all right. Wash your face and go do something else."

26. Find a good doctor and seek professional attention for your depression. You will have weird body issues. Your soul issues will come out in your body tissues! Take the pills along with prayer. Prayer multiplies the power of

the pills. Treat the soul with releasing prayers in this book and your health will resume a lot quicker.

27. Don't be a martyr. Others have suffered trauma too. Don't talk about your loss in a group after the second year. However, you should share your loss to a few close friends and family. Keep your pain from strangers as you would keep a secret. Occasionally, as a need arises, you might mention your situation in general terms. I taught a class and discussed my situation as "family trauma." I was relieved when Dana, a new friend, found out about our loss and said, "Nancy, I never would have known." I believe that's because I was relieved of my bitterness and self-pity by holding on to God and releasing it to Him. I allowed myself to cry and get angry in the solitude of my house, so I didn't carry it out into the world!

28. Resist the temptation to isolate and disconnect from your community. It's natural to want to withdraw, but the word *unity* is in the word *community* for a reason. Stay plugged in to your community, and they will keep you whole and unified.

29. When you get discouraged, encourage someone else! Your child wasn't just your child. They were someone's grandchild, niece, nephew, or cousin. It's good to know you are not alone in the grieving process. Go to lunch with them. You can encourage each other, and they need to be included in some of your healing moments. You can celebrate your child's birthday with family. Go somewhere different for their birthday. Go bowling one year.

30. When you get discouraged, have the courage to call a friend.

31. Remember to say daily, "Hear me, oh Lord, when I cry with my voice. Have mercy also upon me and answer me." (See Psalm 27:7.) First, look for His answers in His Word, the Bible, especially in Psalms. I mean it! The book of Psalms is God's love letter to people who have experienced any sort of trauma. Then you can look in the world around you. Your answer may come in the form of a headline in People Magazine!

32. Forgive God and forgive yourself.

33. Don't unplug from God; He is **your** life support.

34. Don't unplug from your community; you need their unity to stay centered.

35. Treat God the way that you want to be treated.

36. It's ok to be angry, and in the beginning you may want to yell at God, but don't stay there. Be honest about your feelings. **Release** the negative emotions to Him. He knows we can't handle them, but He can. Negative emotions that are stuck in your soul will create body pains and diseases. Negative emotions are like cancer of the soul that can become cancer of the body. I have seen people develop cancer and then repent, forgive, and release the fear, bitterness, anger, hurt, and sorrow onto God, and they become cancer free. (For helpful ideas and materials, visit the websites of Kona Life Church in Kona, HI – konalifechurch.org.)

37. Be sure to end an angry session with a positive statement of hope.

38. Do not let the sun go down on your silent anger. Get it out on the table. He prepares a table in the presence of my enemies. (See Psalm 23.) He takes the vomit out of our soul. He's not put off by our vile remarks. He takes the defiled daggers and makes them divine.

39. For a while, the things that brought me joy before Tommy's death didn't anymore. Doing my favorite things after Tommy died tasted like sawdust. But don't believe the lie that you won't **ever** enjoy them again. It may take a few years, but that favorite activity will resurface.

40. Find a new favorite thing and do it. Sometimes do it with a friend.

41. Don't blame yourself for the trial. Don't blame your spouse. When those thoughts come, whisper a prayer, "Lord, accidents happen. Help me to let go."

42. Replace guilt with something nice you do for yourself or you can do for someone else.

43. If you blame anyone, blame the evil one. There is evil in the world, but don't worry, God has overcome the evil and he will make you and your family whole again. Don't blame God; He is your life support.

44. Don't draw a line to protect your heart. Be brave and let others get close to you.

45. Refuse to be bitter. Live to be better.

46. Live in the present-moment situation. I call it PMS.

47. Men grieve differently than women. It's ok if you cry a lot and he does not.

48. Don't let anything steal your faith. Don't let it out of your grip. Hold onto it for dear life because it is!

49. There is a cloud of many witnesses watching you from heaven. What do you want your child to see you doing? Crying and loving? Crying and hiding? Crying and hating? (The answer is number one.)

50. Push through the pain just like you push through childbirth.

51. Stitch by stitch, your Heavenly Father is using the process of pain to mend your broken heart.

52. When we allow ourselves to grieve, we allow ourselves to heal stitch by stitch. We joined *Grief Share* a wonderful support group for grieving families. WOW! It was awesome. They even have classes for kids where they did crafts. Twelve years later, Mercy still has the things she made.

53. We must let go of the pain by crying with the Lord. See the pain, confusion, and trauma as a big balloon. As we cry with the Good Shepherd, our tears are releasing the balloon toward heaven. Conversely, when we hold onto

the pain by refusing to cry, we are burying the balloon in our soul. If we ignore the balloon (pain) hoping it will go away; the balloon gets bigger and bigger. Eventually it will burst! Sorrow of the soul, if not released to heaven, shows up in the body as pain, sickness, and disease.

54. Let go by crying. If you don't let go, you will carry the pain for the rest of your life. After everyone goes to sleep or goes to school, sit alone with the Good Shepherd. You don't want to be a mental case later in life. You don't want your other children pulling away from you because you refused to deal with today's pain.

55. There is an innate fear of crying. We're afraid if we start crying, we won't quit, or we will break into a million smithereens. There is a right way to cry. If you hold the Lord's hand while you cry, He will pull you up when the tear time is over.

56. It's freeing to know that you don't have to believe in yourself to make it through this process of pain. Believe in your Father God in heaven to get you through. It's freeing to know that you are not trusting in fate. You are trusting in your Father who loves you and gave Himself for you.

57. Start a memento box. I have a large box (72"x16"x16") I keep under our bed. I don't look through it very much, I'm probably too afraid, but at least I have it if I need it. I try to look through it on Valentine's Day and Tommy's birthday. Now it's less than that. I don't know if that is good or bad; it's just what I'm doing.

58.   Make a scrapbook of any time that you had with your child. If you only have an ultrasound picture, frame it and keep it in your bedroom.

59.   Take an interest in heaven! Read as much as you can discover. It is, after all, the place where your child is spending all his time. Read to your children about heaven. Your kids can talk about heaven every day. I think it helps them set their priorities in a higher place. They won't live for meaningless material possessions but for eternal reward. Thinking about heaven will cause them to look at life's trials as speed bumps along the journey of life.

60.   Don't worry about your kids during this trial, but do pray for them. Prayer can become a worry wart list, so stay positive by praying the promises of God not the problems. Take your kids to a good Christian counselor that has a lot of experience with the death of a sibling, who can especially help your kids with fear and confusion. For little children, pray for good teachers and God's peace to surround them. For teen children, thank God for diverting their eyes away from temptation and onto Him. God has a calling and a destiny on their lives. Trust Him to make it happen. Ask Him every day to make it happen. He **will** pull them through. He will never ever give up on them.

61.   Teach your kids what you are learning about healing. Possibly teach them the prescriptions of this book. They are never too young to plug into God. He is their Father in heaven. Expect God to speak to you through your kids.

Believe them. They may be honestly blunt, but don't get hurt. Take their messages to heart. Use their comments as if they were a megaphone from heaven, and ask God to help you do whatever suggestions your kids have.

62. Keep your prayers simple and make sure they reflect honestly how you feel. Always end your honest prayer sessions with a statement of **hope**.

63. When I miss Tommy so much, I ask God to give him a present from me. It's usually something big and extravagant like a tractor, an elephant, sterling silver tea service with heavenly hot chocolate which is, believe it or not, better than Angelina's hot chocolate from Paris.

    Your kids can do the same thing. They can draw a picture and ask God to take a photo of it and show it to your child in heaven.

64. Meditate on this amazing (and my favorite) promise. Read it slowly, out loud, and consider what God is saying to you through these verses.

    Trust in the LORD with all your heart
    And do not lean on your own understanding.
    In all your ways acknowledge Him,
    And He will make your paths straight.
    Do not be wise in your own eyes;
    Fear the Lord and turn away from evil.
    It will be healing to your body
    And refreshment to your bones.
    Honor the Lord from your wealth

And from the first of all your produce;
So your barns will be filled with plenty
And your vats will overflow with new wine.
(Proverbs 3:5-10 NASB)

SIMPLE PRAYERS
(As written in the chapters of this book)

Day 9 – Prayer of Beginning

"God of Heaven, I choose this day to give You a chance in my life. I want to start believing that You are a merciful and kind God. I am sorry for thinking You were bad and mean. Thank You, that I don't have to be perfect or have it all together before You will love me. You love me just the way I am and just because I am Your child. Thank You God that You promise that if I draw near to You, You will draw close to me. Wrap Yourself around me, my husband, and my other children. Teach them Your ways and give them Your truth which is the foundation of real, lasting peace."

Day 11 – Prayer of a Lamb

"Dear Good Shepherd, take me in Your arms and hold me as a little lamb. Hold me close and don't let me go. Don't let me succumb to my dark moments, and don't let my family out of Your sight! Teach me Your ways, and lead my family and me on the level path that You have laid out for us. Blow through my spirit, soul, and body, and remove all the fog. Wash my mind of any doubt and confusion. Fill me with Your hope, strength, and courage. If You are with me, I can make it."

Day 22 - Prayer for Anger

"Dear God, I am so fighting mad at You! I didn't even get to _____ with my child! I was planning to _____ with them! Now I'll never get to _____ with them. Nevertheless, You hold the words of eternal life and there is no one like You. I don't want to live alone, slugging through life. I choose to believe that You love me and will explain everything when I see You. In the meantime, I am looking forward to _____ with my child in heaven."

Day 25 - Prayer for Dread

"I am so weak that I don't think I can even tie my own shoes. Give me Your strength for the small daily things. There are so many things that I dread! Inject into my heart Your courage. Give me Your grace and peace so that I don't have to rush into everything related to life. I am so scared, Lord. Fill the void that is in my heart without _____ with Your perfect, divine love. (Be still and wait for Him to fill you.) Fill...Fill... Fill... Touch my family the way You're touching me. Heal us spirit, soul, and body."

Day 26 – Prayer of Trusting Him to Bring Vision

"How could You let this happen? You are supposed to protect us. Where were You? Heavenly Father, I am so confused and angry. I know I can't hold this in, or I will explode. So clean me out God. I release all today's anger and bitterness to You. (Breathe out.) Take it all. I don't want it. (Try to imagine today's anger evaporating away.) I don't like what happened, but I am going to trust that You will work the bad situation into good. Give me eyes to see, ears to hear, and a heart to perceive that You are with me and that I am not walking alone. Open my ears to hear Your still, small, sweet voice. Open my mouth to speak the truth in love. Open my eyes to see Your path that You have set out for me. Help me to perceive Your ways."

Day 29 – Prayer for Exchanging Fear for His Love

"Lord, disconnect me from all fear that makes me live in a constant state of performance and perfection. Take me off the treadmill. Wrap Yourself around me, and infuse into every cell of my spirit, soul, and body that I am accepted by You, my Heavenly Daddy. Make me have a Mary heart. Reveal to me that being loved and mesmerized by You is the only really important thing that matters. Show me how to change my habits and to walk in Your ways of joy and peace."

Day 30 – Prayer for Hearing His Voice and Your Name

"Lord, take the new sorrows and restlessness in my heart and replace them with Your contentment and peace. Help me to hear Your voice that is still, small, and sweet. I want to hear You say my name. Make me like Mary, and help me to be looking up to You and not at my troubles. Replace any worries I have with Your faith."

Day 34 and 35 – Prayer for Renouncing Fear

"Good Shepherd, I do not want to live in fear anymore. I renounce fear and all its torment over me and my family. I ask You, Lord, to remove every trace of fear from my spirit, soul, and body. Inject into every cell of my being Your power, Your love, and Your sound mind. I give You permission to dismantle the work of fear in my life. Separate me from any family tendency toward fear. Today, I set up a new foundation of faith in You."

Day 36 – Prayer for Sleeping

"I will lay down in peace and sleep, for Thou, oh Lord, will make sure that I dwell in safety. I am not alone. You are with me, and You never sleep or slumber. From now on, You are the one who goes before me and my family. I ask that You assign angels over me and my children: an angel on our left and an angel on our right. You will not leave me or forsake me. You are our fortress and strong tower. You are our safe place because You have wrapped Your eternal arms of strength around me. I will trust You."

Day 40 – Prayer for Your Children

May my children (list them by name) walk with You. May they be who You created them to be. May they lead others into Your Kingdom. Help them to grow in discernment. May they run from impurity and stand up for righteousness. May they grow in Your wisdom and in their authority in You, while retaining a submissive and humble spirit. May they find their identity in You.

Day 41 – Prayer for Marriage

"Good Shepherd, my marriage needs You right now. If You come and hold both of us, I know we'll make it. Open our eyes to see each other's needs. Open our hearts to see each other's hurts. Help us to prefer each other. Do not let envy or strife get a foot in the door. Stop selfishness and self- pity in its tracks. Help us to prefer each other more than ourselves. Change us so we desire to listen more than to be heard."

Day 43 – Prayer of Trust and Understanding

"Lord, now I understand that You aren't jealous like a man; You are jealous **for** my happiness! Establish Your presence in me and let Your Presence bring peace to my spirit, soul, and body. Lord, help me to trust You even when I don't see or understand the plan. Thank You that I don't have to do live alone. You are with me and walking in my every footprint. Live and breathe through me. Be in my heart, my feet, my hands. Help me to see that You delight in me just the way I am."

Day 49 – Prayer for Grief and Sorrow

"Lord, nothing makes sense anymore. Everything that I thought was truth got rocked. Help me to hold on to You for dear life! Lord, remove all **confusion** from my spirit, soul and body. I release it to You now. (Breathe in and out.) Lift the fog off my mind. Give me Your clarity and understanding. Bring my body, my heart, my lungs, my immune system, my chemistry, my _____ into Your perfect, divine order. Break the stronghold that grief and sorrow have over my life and my family. Push today's anxiety away from me. **Impart Your resurrection life** into my innermost being. Deposit hope into the core of my being. Plant the seed of Your amazing love into every cell of my spirit, soul, and body, and make it grow in exponential ways. Blow Your Life into the places that are dark and sad and lifeless. I receive Your shield of grace and the light of Your protection."

Day 50 – Prayer of Admittance

"God of the Universe, help me not to deny my pain but to bring it to You. Give me the courage to take off any masks that I am clinging to. I need You just to make it through one day. Transfer

Your strength and refreshing into me. I surrender to You. I depend on You. Let Your presence flow in around me and my family today. Be the strength of my family. Be my family's rock to lean on. Be real to them."

Day 51 – Prayer of Strength

"Lord of all the heavens, I am running on empty. Be my strength today. Let Your power pulsate through me. I need Your presence because You are the source of life and goodness. Refresh my spirit, soul, and body. Wash over me. Heal my heart and mind. Only You, can help me keep calm and carry on."

Day 52 – Prayer for Broken-Heartedness

"Father God, I am missing _____ so much that my heart literally hurts. Thank You for being near to the broken-hearted. Bind up my broken heart. (In your mind's eye, see Him binding your broken heart.) Thank You that You won't turn me away. You are the Healer. Wrap Your Spirit around me with the comfort of Your love. There is such a void without my child. Would You come and fill the void that I feel? Fill me. Fill me. Fill me to overflowing."

Day 54 – Prayer for Vision

"Give me eyes to see, ears to hear, and a heart to perceive that You are with me and that I am not walking alone. Shine Your light so that I don't grope in the darkness. Open my ears to hear Your still, small, sweet voice. Open my mouth to speak the truth in love. Open my eyes to see Your path that You have set out for me. Help me to perceive Your ways. Awaken me to feel alive again."

Day 56 – Prayer for Emotions

"Father God, I feel like I am falling. Hold me! Hug Me! Here I am again with so much pain that I could burst. I release it to You. (Imagine it evaporating out of you.) Lord, where I have shut down my emotions, gradually help me to feel again. Where my emotions are out of control, stop them with the force of Your peace. Cause my emotions to be transformed into productivity. Help me to trust You and know that I don't have to be perfect even in my grieving. Heal me through and through. Renew my heart, body, and mind into perfect wholeness and happiness."

Day 57 – Prayer for Shock and Trauma

"Lord, cause all shock and trauma to be released out of my spirit, soul, and body. Take every trace of confusion out of me, and renew my spirit, soul, and body to wholeness and happiness as You originally designed. Where my body glands, chemistry, or immune system is out of whack, command it to align into Your perfect order and balance. Release Your glory and light into my life. Lead me in Your love forevermore. Thank You that You promise to work things together for good."

Day 58 – Prayer of Release

"Lord of heaven, I need Your presence because You are the source of life and goodness. Refresh my spirit, soul, and body. Wash over me. Heal my heart and mind. By your authority, stop the compulsive thoughts that keep coming into my mind, or show me the root cause. I release my worries of _____. I release fears of _____. I release my bitterness tied to _____. You said to give You all my trouble. So I take this log off my shoulder, and I give it to You. Deliver me from all negative tendencies that I inherited from my family such as bitterness, worrying, or being fearful. I choose to lift up my eyes towards heaven, because my help comes from You, the maker of heaven and earth."

Day 63 – Prayer for Confusion and Shame

"Daddy God, I was so shocked and embarrassed and confused that my child's life ended like this! Help me to get through all of this. Lift me above the floodwaters of confusion. (See Him lifting you and your family up.) Command all effects of shock and trauma to come out of my spirit, soul, and body. Use Your power to remove all confusion and to make me normal again in my body and soul. Rebuke the shadow of death and suicide around me and my family. I release all shame to You. Be the shade on my right hand, and don't let me feel stares and judgment. Help me to feel the truth that most good-hearted people have love and concern for me. I don't want to live in paranoia or be over-protective about my other children. Make the torment of fear dissolve under the power of Your love. Send the Comforter to wrap me in peace so I can finally rest. Fill me with Your joy which gives me strength."

Day 64 – Prayer for Simple Faith

"Heavenly Father, I choose to trust You with a simple trust. I open the door wide to You! There are so many questions, but it doesn't matter, because You are the answer. I release all my fears to You. Any fear that is bound up in me, let it be loosed off of me. (Breathe out and in.) Give me abiding, consistent, living, faith that comes from my heart, not my head. I want to relax in my faith, which will bring a peace to my body and soul. Wrap me in Your counsel and correction. I don't want to grope in the darkness like a blind woman. Take my hand, and surround me and my family with the light of Your life."

Day 74 – Prayer of Newness with God

"God, why do I have trouble trusting You? Who do I need to forgive? (He might bring a person to mind that wounded you.) I forgive _____ for hurting me and for giving me a wrong message about You. Disconnect me from this anger and all wrong messages I have believed about You. You hold the words and power that will heal me, and there is no one like You. I don't want to live alone, slugging through life. Dear Heavenly Father, I choose to "forgive You" for _____ and believe that You are good, kind, and faithful. You will never leave me. (In your mind's eye, let the Good Shepherd give you a new picture of Him with you so you have a true message about who He is.) In the meantime, I am looking forward to doing _____ with my child in heaven."

Day 75 – Prayer of Anger toward God

"I hate you! I release all my anger to You. I don't want to hold onto any of this anger. I give it all to You. (Breathe out and take a few minutes to release your emotion.) Thank You that You even allow me to be honest with You, and You won't abandon me."

Day 79 – Establish Your Presence

"Lord, establish Your presence in me, and let Your presence bring peace to my spirit, soul, and body. Lord, help me to trust You even in hard times. Help me to trust You when I don't see or understand the plan. Let me not rely on my own strength and the arm of the flesh but on Your ability and power. Lord grant rest to my soul. Lord, I receive the anointing of life to overcome the works of death and destruction in my life. I receive the goodness of Your glory. Today, I will factor the power of God into my life. Holy Spirit, activate the supernatural in my life. Give me revelation of Your truth and let this bring freedom to my spirit, soul, and body."

Day 80 – Prayer for Bitterness

"Lord God, I choose to receive Your grace and mercy. (Take several deep breaths.) Show me where I am carrying anger and bitterness. (Wait for Him to show you.) I release this anger about _____ to You right now. I don't want to spiral out of control. Hold me tightly. Wrap me in forgiveness, and lead me in Your goodness. Release Your glory. Lead me in Your love forevermore. Heavenly Father, impart Your resurrection life into my innermost being. Deposit Your hope into the core of my being. Plant the seed of Your perfect love into every cell of my spirit, soul, and body, and make it grow in exponential ways."

Day 82 - Prayer for Hopelessness

"I had a new sadness hit me today. (Breathe out.) Lord, I release this sadness to You. I release hopelessness to You. Hold me tight! Establish my family in Your love. Pump Your resurrection life into my family and fill us with Your peace that passes my understanding. Infuse hope into the cells of my spirit, soul, and body. Fill me with the force of Your life. Heal me inside out. Make all of my disorders be dissolved by Your love."

Day 83 – Prayer for Breaking Strongholds

"Father God, open the windows of my soul and let Your light of life blow through my soul. Do some house cleaning! Blow on me,

God. Touch me and give me Your courage to do this! Forgive me for pride, anger, and judgment. I renounce them. I forgive the drunk driver, insurance companies, doctors that I felt could have done more, my boss, my husband, my child for _____ (drinking on the night he died, etc.), and the church. I "forgive" You, God, and I forgive myself. I release blame out of my spirit, soul, and body. Father, get rid of any trace of self-blame. You have to do it. (Squeeze the Good Shepherd's hand.) I bless my enemies and their families, businesses, and lives. Heavenly Father, disconnect me and my family from all negative and wrong tendencies we inherited from our ancestral lineage. Superimpose Your perfect DNA on my family so we can carry out Your destiny on the earth without any hindrances. Fill my parched heart with your Holy liquefying presence. Open a valve in my spirit, soul, and body to release all the stress and pressure that I am carrying. Fill my entire being with Your power, love, and sound mind."

Day 86 – Prayer of Feeling Betrayed

"Daddy, I need Your help to remove this excruciating pain that is my heart and back. Send Your angels to help me. I renounce all feelings related to betrayal out of my spirit, soul, and body. Help me, Lord, if I leave anything out. I release all hurt, all betrayal, all shock, all worthlessness, all inferiority, all bewilderment, and all confusion out of my soul and body. I choose to believe that I have Your undivided attention and love. I also release all envy, all jealousy, and all bitterness about _____ to You right now that is related to friends that still have their children. Wash that junk out of me as I wash my soul with my tears. I release and let go of feeling unloved, forgotten, abandoned, and rejected. I release feeling like an orphan to You, Heavenly Father. If I picked up any self-pity or martyr-likeness along the way, I give that to You too. I don't want this junk anymore. I don't want to live like this anymore. I renounce and disconnect from all these false feelings. I throw them on the ground! I step on them now! Heavenly Father, take all this stuff **away** from me and throw it in the pit.

Heavenly Father, I have dried my eyes and with conviction in my heart, I have decided to put on these new clothes instead. I choose to put on Your blouse of loveliness, the vest of worthiness, the skirt of faithfulness, the necklace of redemption, the scarf of contentment, and the earrings of acceptance. One earring is Your acceptance of me, and the other is acceptance of myself. To all of these things I add the belt of truth, to tie everything together. No outfit would be complete without the sandals of assurance that say, 'I am Your beloved daughter.' If You are a King, that makes me a princess! Wow! Heavenly Father, thank You for loving me unconditionally. Thank You for adopting me into Your family. Thank You for truly caring about me and my family. I **love** You!"

Day 89 – Prayer of Closure

"God You are so wonderful! You are better than I ever imagined. My whole life I was afraid of You, and now at the worst time in my life, I discover that You are good, kind, and faithful. Lift me up to Your throne room. I give You all the regrets I have related to my child's death. (See yourself giving Him your regrets.) Heal me through and through. Heavenly Father, stop the train of thoughts with the power of Your peace. Touch my kids. Keep them out of trouble. Give them divine appointments with people who will lead them to a closer walk with You. Tell my child in heaven that I miss them and that I am sending them a letter. Tell them that I am not mad anymore. Tell them that I totally and completely forgive them! Tell them to enjoy their new life and build me a _____. Thank You for completely loving me, faults and all. I love You, Lord. I love You. I love You."

Day 90 - Prayer of Release

"Dear Lord, I release to You all my pain, all my grief, and all my sorrow and confusion. I release it new every day. Let it float out of me like balloons. I send it all to You. I release any regrets, any blame, any shame to You. Wash Your love over me.

"Give me Your wisdom and strength to keep the faith in You and Your goodness. Shine Your Light on me. Drive away the darkness I feel. Don't let the spirit of heaviness consume me. Fill me with faith in You, hope in future, and love for myself, others, and especially, You, God.

"Hold me when I cry. I hold You in one hand, and when sadness comes, I will cry with You because You will not let me break into a zillion little pieces.

"Reveal Your perfect plan for me and my family. Fill me with Your courage, Your wisdom, and knowledge to accomplish all that You want me to do. Give me eyes to see, ears to hear, and a heart to perceive Your love and truth.

"I declare, 'God, You will give me a good life here on this earth if I keep following You.'

"Thank You for adopting me into Your kingdom and family. I gladly accept being Your daughter, which is crazy because that means I am a princess!"